FAMILY HISTORY, MODERN GENETICS, AND WELL-
KEPT SECRETS COLLIDE AS ANGIE BIER IS
DRAWN INTO A SEARCH FOR A STRANGER'S
BIRTH FATHER HIDDEN SOMEWHERE IN HER
OWN FAMILY TREE. THE SEARCH LEADS TO
DUSTY ARCHIVES, CLUES HIDDEN IN PLAIN SIGHT,
AND THE CUTTING EDGE OF COMMERCIAL
GENETIC TESTING.

Fifty-something Kathleen used 23andme to identify her biological mother, who is rumored to have a child with a priest. Kathleen believes that her father is Angie's great-uncle Ed, a beloved monsignor. Angie's genealogy and medical backgrounds balk at this conclusion. Couldn't it be one of the other seven priests in the family?

Despite initial reluctance, she is drawn full force into the mystery. Angie visits archives around Wisconsin, creating dossiers on the potential priest fathers. Kathleen discovers articles online with tantalizing clues hidden in plain sight. Angie's geneticist sister applies modern techniques to unravel this complex case of genetic genealogy.

After a year, Angie determines that a distant relative is Kathleen's and Henry's father. They work together to sketch out their biological parents' story, one wound up in expectations, disappointments, and secrets hidden in plain sight. As they arrive at answers, new questions continue to surface and each struggles to craft a narrative that answers them fully. Ultimately, they create a new definition of family and celebrate it with all of its amazing twists and turns.

Early Praise for The Accidental Archivist

The Accidental Archivist is a delicious combination of memoir, sleuthing, and family secrets. Written with deep compassion, but also an overwhelming sense of curiosity and a need to know the truth, Bier digs through relationships and family history, putting beloved dots together in a different pattern. Facts grow from multi-generational lore, creating a new picture in the family album.--**Kathie Giorgio, author of *All Told* and *If You Tame Me***

Angela Bier's *The Accidental Archivist* is a personal, true mystery story. Genealogist by hobby, Bier pursues the unknown background of a relative's parentage, particularly the father. While tracing family trees could be monotonous, Bier brings both variety and humor to her account, using emails, letters, photos, and dialogue. For anyone who enjoys stories of family dynamics and mysteries, Bier's tale can be a compelling one.-**Mary Ann Noe, author of *To Know Her* and *A Handful of Pearls* Accidental**

Accidental Archivist is a uniquely fascinating mushup of mystery and memoir. It travels down the path of a clouded family history and attempts to lift the fog on a scandalous story of a distant ancestor. Along the way, exhaustive research ranges from interpreting personal letters and photographs, to interesting revelations found using DNA testing. Bier's quest for the truth takes us into a detective story that wades through hunches, conjecture and blind alleys in search of answers to a long-held family secret. Bier's debut is a wild swing through the branches of a family tree!—**Jim Landwehr, author of *Dirty Shirt, The Portland House, Cretin Boy* and *At the Lake.***

Nowadays, genealogists have genetics thrown into the mix. When disagreements crop up between traditional records and genetic data, I embrace them. Why might someone give their child up for adoption? Why might a woman lie about the paternity of her child? The discrepancies tell a truth in their own right

The Accidental Archivist

Angela Bier

Moonshine Cove Publishing, LLC

Abbeville, South Carolina U.S.A.

First Moonshine Cove Edition June 2022

ISBN: 9781952439353

Library of Congress LCCN: 202210724

Cover by Patrick Bier, interior design by Moonshine Cove staff.

About the Author

Angie is a former pediatrician, mother, community activist, and an accomplished amateur genealogist. Her writing career

was launched when she won the "Little House, Big Story" prize for her Laura Ingalls Wilder inspired essay, "The Reason Why." Her writing can be found most recently in *Evening Street Review* and her upcoming young adult novel, *Voices.* She is a student of AllWriters Workplace & Workshop, LLC, and lives in Franklin, Wisconsin, with her husband, two daughters, and dog.

angelabier.com

Acknowledgments

Thanks to Kathleen and Henry, for allowing me to tag along on their story and share it with the world; to my family, Jimmy, Natalie & Evelyn, for their patience and support as I "spend [sometimes] too much time with dead people;" to my friends at AllWriters, for somehow convincing me that I am a writer; to my writing coach, cheerleader, and sometime therapist, Kathie; to my book club friends, Vicky, Patty, Leah, Michelle, and Julie, for being the first 'outsiders' to read and love this book--your enthusiasm meant so much to me; to Mom and Grandma Bier who hung out with me in the dusty stacks and cemeteries and taught me to see the amazing stories contained therein; to my sister Louise, who dropped her life to participate in yet another sisterly adventure.

To Kathleen & Henry

Author's Note

The people and circumstances in this story are real. Where I was not present for events, I imagined scenes to fill in the blanks. For the most part, though, the amazing story that landed in my lap is true. The sketch map below shows the location of places mentioned as this story unfolded.

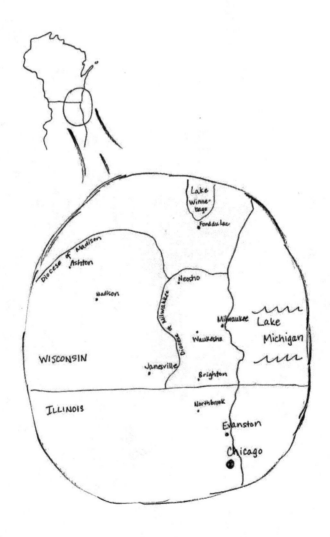

THE ACCIDENTAL ARCHIVIST

Prologue

Kathleen pulled out her tablet and settled it on the cafe table. She gazed out at the waves of the southern California coastline and tried to allow their rhythm to calm her mind. She needed to address the hornet nest that her cousin, Liz, inadvertently kicked over. Liz was a relatively newish cousin, and Kathleen was still finding her way with her. She only incorporated Liz into her own life story a few years back, during the search for her birth mother. They found each other on the DNA analysis site, 23andme. Kathleen had plenty of lifelong first cousins and siblings back in Chicago growing up, but none to whom she was actually related in a blood sense. She and Liz corresponded feverishly in those early days, until they unraveled the mystery of who her mother was and assigned her a name—Ginny Roethle. Liz proved a more than worthy sidekick in her ongoing search for more details of her birth story—she was an amateur genealogist and well-versed in Roethle family lore. She would always love Liz for helping to give her Ginny.

But sometimes Liz's enthusiasm got a little ahead of itself. Once the two of them further determined that Kathleen's birth father was likely a priest, she knew that they needed to tread lightly with further inquiries. Through 23andme's data, she had a hunch that her priest father lurked somewhere in the branches of a sprawling Wisconsin family tree with the amusing surname "Bier"—German for beer. What an amazing stroke of luck, then, when Liz directed her to a genealogy colleague who blogged on both the Roethle and the Bier family histories! Kathleen particularly enjoyed the blogger's entries on a family excursion to the Bier family homeland in Germany and the Czech Republic. She read the entries hungrily and studied the pictures with amusement—they looked like a fun crowd. She still wasn't certain how this blogger, Angie Bier was her name, could possibly be related to both the Bier and the Roethle families, the same as she was. It was all a bit confusing to Kathleen's stereotypically left-brained psyche. But Liz reassured her that it made sense. Especially if her suspicions about the priest father's identity were correct. Maybe this Angie could be instrumental in her search for her biological father.

Kathleen commented favorably on the blog and introduced herself in an initial letter. She let the blogger know about her Roethle connection on her biological mother's side. She planned to do a bit more research and bide her time before broaching the subject of an unfaithful Bier priest as her father. But as soon as the blogger returned from her trip and responded to her message, a cc'd Liz dropped the bomb. Without warning her, Liz sent a message to this mysterious Angie, loaded with all of the facts, suppositions, and innuendos in one tidy, explosive package. Kathleen wasn't surprised when Liz forwarded Angie's subsequent response, which amounted to: "Sorry, can't help you there. Good luck, don't call us, we'll call you."

Sigh.

She tied her dark hair back into a ponytail, took a sip of her latte, and got to work writing another letter to this random blogger in Wisconsin. She needed to be non-threatening, but curious. She needed her to know that she didn't want scandals, just a few answers. Some of Kathleen's friends, and even her children, suggested that she just lay off. Wasn't the information about her biological mother enough? After all, she had a pretty nice life going for her in San Clemente. Why keep digging for ghosts in the frigid Midwest? Kathleen couldn't provide neat answers, and instead tended to demur with phrases about "just wanting answers," and "needing medical information." Really? Despite living in the most populated metropolis in the U.S., with a husband and three adult children nearby, she just wanted to stop feeling alone. She pushed back her sleeves and got to work.

From: Kathleen LeFranc
To: Angela Bier

Dear Angela . . .

Chapter One
The General

The comforter in the Munich hotel room was a feat of German engineering. It was thick without being heavy, and the housekeeping staff changed the duvet cover daily. Collapsing into bed that night, I was content, exhausted and still a little bit nervous. I was the self-appointed leader for an excursion of 17 Bier family members to The German Homeland, a two weeklong dream trip we talked about for years. We were all descendants of Valentine Bier, an ethnic German who emigrated to southern Wisconsin with his wife and seven children in 1882. We were making the reverse voyage, not out of economic dire straits, but curiosity. Our motley group of Valentine descendants ranged in age from my dad at 66 down to a cousin, 17. They all entrusted their time and money on a trip that hinged on my good planning.

With the assistance of a wonderful travel agent and my own ruthless efficiency, it all came together in the end. Months of planning, a dozen spreadsheets, and countless emails later, the Biers were in Munich, the first leg of the ten-day trip. I put together an itinerary catering to varied tastes and we traveled by mini bus through two countries. At times in the preceding year and a half of planning, it didn't seem possible. But now, as I leaned out my window, overlooking the Munich train station and watched the backpackers and business people scurrying about in the fading summer sun, it was deliciously real.

Our family's last name, "Bier," is German for, well, beer. My clan knew we were in for a memorable trip when our guide at arrivals attracted a crowd with her "Bier Trip" sign. Who wouldn't want to join that party? Similarly, a quick flash of a U.S. driver's license sporting the name "Bier" always served as a handy conversation starter. The entire desk staff at the hotel knew us and were fans of our name. The concierge was palpably confused when I explained that people back home were often reluctant to pronounce our last name correctly; they were afraid of offending us by calling us after the beverage. "Why would they think beer was bad?" the confused woman wondered.

My boisterous uncle pulled out his driver's license so many times to flash his name that I contemplated getting him a lanyard for more ready access. This name game was performed to greatest effect that evening at the Hofbräuhaus. Being a requisite tourist landmark, it was super crowded and it seemed a hopeless task to seat all of us together. However, my uncle leveraged the name to score us a table in the impossibly crowded courtyard. Additionally, he kindled a new friendship with a local beer/bier lover, clad questionably in denim lederhosen. The evening culminated in shared beers, gingerbread hearts, and hearty handshakes.

I have so much affection for my name that I didn't change it when I married ten years ago, despite having seriously considered doing so. I usually explain that my husband's Korean-American last name, Kim, didn't match me and my blonde hair. But the real reason? I simply couldn't bear to change. I'm a Bier, always have been, always will be. The difference in surnames between me and our two daughters caused occasional confusion with their school. But for the most part, it didn't raise any eyebrows. Indeed, my home state of Wisconsin has such deep German roots that the Bier name carries almost as much cache there as it did in Germany itself. Once people learn how to pronounce it correctly, that is.

No one was surprised that I became the trip's self-appointed leader. Growing up as the eldest of five siblings, my nickname was, and remains, "The General." I love nothing more than a spreadsheet, a bulleted list, and a plan coming together. When I was eleven, I actually catalogued and created check-out cards for my entire childhood library, including all 35 of the original *Baby Sitters Club* books. Shockingly, no one ever stopped by to peruse the library, my childhood home being surrounded by Southern Wisconsin corn and soybean fields rather than neighbors. But boy, were those books organized.

This natural inclination to organize led to my becoming head genealogist and archivist for all branches of my family tree—organization skills and the fact that I was drawn to the stories in my Grandma Bier's genealogy books. She had the bug too, and I loved convincing her to crack out the genealogy albums. When she grew elderly and was ready to pass on her work, I was the natural recipient. When a person such as me exists in a family, the question of "what do we do with THAT box of stuff?" always has a ready answer—give it to Angie! Reams of paper, photographs in various stages of repair, hanks of first-haircut hair, boxes of baby teeth—I've unpacked 'em all. I take the treasures through a series of steps, carefully honed over years of practice and reading on archival practices.

First, determine what to save. Remove the item from the uniformly inappropriate storage medium in which it is currently housed. Note any significant genealogical data in a database. Create a digital copy of the item. Securely store the original in the appropriate container. Pore over the digital copies and think about their significance. How could I best tell this object's story? Where did it fit in the larger story of the family? How would I ever have enough time to work on all the projects that I dreamed up?

People give family history only a passing glance. Me? I just couldn't look away. I was probably meant to practice some sort of ancestor worship instead of being raised Catholic. Somehow, by arranging those names and dates and ordering them and, if possible, assigning them stories—I believed it kept those people's spirits alive. There are few things more pathetic than a box of old studio portraits for sale at a rummage sale, rendered nameless because no one bothered to treasure them.

In all of the accidental archives that I accumulated, the diaries reigned supreme. First hand, original, handwritten diaries of the Bier family dating back to the late 1800s. In these primary sources, the authors wrote of banal, everyday events. But between those lines, I traced out the story of where the Valentine Bier family came from with, at times, stunning detail. House number 78, Ketzelsdorf, Bohemia.

With that starting information and some luck, I identified the exact location of this little village. That's what the name Ketzelsdorf means: shortened village. Legend has it that it was originally called Langendorf, or long village, before a huge fire led to its final name.

Ketzelsdorf, or Koclirov as it is now known, lay nestled on the border between the regions of Bohemia and Moravia in what is now the Czech Republic. I designed our trip to begin in Munich to get a bit of German history and flavor, and then move into Prague, and ultimately the Bohemian countryside. I hoped to get some answers about what the family was up to before emigrating, take some pictures, and generally soak up the place. Oh, yes. And blog about the trip. My blog was a haphazard collection of memoirs, everyday observations, and genealogy. I started it a few years before the trip. During the trek, I used the site to share exhaustive details for the interested family back home.

After I finished up that day's entry, I was tired and wanted nothing more than to sink into the comforter. It was midnight, and we had a full day of sightseeing ahead of us. I blinked my eyes open and forced myself to read and respond to the handful of comments that accumulated during the past 24 hours. Blogging family history and travel on this trip brought out a lot more views and comments than usual, and I wanted to respond in kind. I scanned and found a commenter who was new to me, a Kathleen. My eyes quickly read the message and zeroed in one key phrase:

I am part of your family.

Huh.

From: Kathleen LeFranc
To: Me

Angie, I was born in October, 1952, and I'm adopted. I was raised in Chicago. I went through ancestry.com and 23andMe and have found first cousins. I am part of your family. My grandmother is Helen Bier who married Leo Roethle and her daughter Virginia Roethle, who died when she was 68 in 2001, is my mother. I've met several wonderful cousins in this search, so I have already been fortunate to learn a lot about the family history. I hope we have an opportunity to chat.

An adopted-away relative. Interesting—the first that I was aware of. There were a handful of Bier and Roethle relatives that were adopted *into* the family, but this was the first I heard of the other direction. I wasn't surprised, though. For one thing, in a family the size of mine, the odds of a young woman discreetly surrendering a child to adoption were high. For another thing, I constantly met "new to me" relatives that previously flew under the radar. If anyone ever asked if I was related to "So-and-so Bier" that they met somewhere in southern Wisconsin, my answer was always "Yes." If they were a Bier from southern Wisconsin, we were related. I could quickly trace back to a common relative with my genealogy software.

This Kathleen's email mentioned not one, but two, names from my dad's side of the family, Bier and Roethle. I assumed she was correct in claiming membership in the clan, with the adoption twist. I was intrigued. That night, though, I was also preoccupied and exhausted. So, I wrote quick reply and added her email to my "genealogy: to do" file. Ruthless efficiency at work, even while on vacation.

* * *

A month or so later, the trip was over. All expectations for a fulfilling reconnection with the Bier natal roots were exceeded. I was content. I rested on my laurels for a few weeks, and then life quickly returned to normal. One day, I pulled up Kathleen's email, along with all the rest that accumulated in my "genealogy: to do" file. These messages ranged from invitations from long-lost cousins to meet for coffee, to requests for copies of family group sheets.

A review of Kathleen's facts proved to be in line with my own: My great-grandmother, Rosalie Roethle, and Kathleen's biological grandfather, Leo Roethle, were siblings. Leo Roethle married Helen Bier, and Rosalie married Edward Bier-explaining the parallel Bier and

Roethle connections. I checked my genealogy contact sheet and found a woman from that branch that I'd written last about ten years previous. I hoped she was still alive. Her name was Liz, and she would have been Kathleen's first cousin. Before sharing any more with Kathleen, I needed to make sure that Liz knew of her newfound biological cousin. To be fair, I also wanted to make sure that Kathleen was on the up-and-up. Liz quickly responded in the affirmative to both questions. So, I went ahead and wrote back to Kathleen:

From: Me
Date: Kathleen LeFranc, Liz M.

Hi, Kathleen—
Believe it or not, I just got back! Right after completing the trip to Europe, we took a vacation with my in-laws. Whew, what a summer. I talked to Liz just to make sure that SHE was aware of you, so it sounds like you've already made contact with her. I don't know a lot about the Roethle family. It seems like most of the family didn't have kids. I do hope to do a brief blog synopsis of that branch of the family tree in the future, so stay tuned. Unfortunately, I don't have any photos of your mother either.

What are your cousins like? Have you been to Wisconsin?

Angie

I pulled up my genealogy management software and made a note of the continuation of Virginia Roethle's line with Kathleen McHugh LeFranc. Virginia was a "dead end," having no children of which anyone was previously aware. I added Kathleen as a daughter with no father attached. My tree is modest in size—2,481 individuals with the addition of Kathleen. Some die-hard genealogists sport trees numbering into the tens of thousands. I grew my tree by one, and didn't give Kathleen LeFranc much more thought. She seemed pleasant, she read the blog, and I had one more contact to squirrel away.

The next morning, I flicked open my laptop. I was surprised to see a message in my inbox, not from Kathleen, but from her cousin, Liz.

From: Liz M.
To: Me

Angie -
It's so nice to talk to you again!!
I need to ask you a question. It involves Kathleen and her 50-year search for her biological parents. DNA proves she is my first cousin and a photo confirmed she is Virginia Roethle's daughter. She looks just like her mother. Since I was born in 1950, I was old enough to know that Virginia had a baby that she gave up for adoption. I was also aware that Virginia, as a 19-year old girl, got pregnant by a priest. Our family knew that. Virginia was taken to Illinois to live with a family while pregnant. Kathleen was able to find a member of that family who confirmed that Virginia lived there with them while pregnant and they also knew that the father was a priest.

This is the hard part. My memories and conclusions indicate that Kathleen's father was Fr. Ed Bier, who would have been 30 years old. Kathleen doesn't want anything, other than to know who she is. No trouble or turmoil or anything like that. She's a real nice person, smart, sharp — she said she would have loved to go on the trip to Europe with the Biers. My question to you is...have you or anyone in your family ever heard this, too? About Fr. Ed?

Liz

Um...in a word, no. I hadn't even thought about Father Ed in years. Where did Liz come up with this crazy theory? And what of the mysterious Kathleen? So much for a benign, interesting correspondence. I felt myself immediately slip to the defensive, drafting a "don't call us, we'll call you," brush-off email.

Koclirov, a.k.a., Ketzelsdorf. Postcard-perfect Bohemian village.

Chapter Two
Father Ed

Before he was Father Ed, Ed Bier was just one of The Four Bier Boys. These four grew up on the Bier home farm on the fertile, flat lands of the poorly-named Rock Prairie of Wisconsin. They worked hard, helping their dad to run the farm that he inherited from his own father, the original immigrant to Wisconsin from Bohemia. But when they weren't working? They played hard. Beer, football, cards—all of it. They were a scrappy, troublesome lot, and three of the four of them produced large numbers of scrappy, troublesome children. The majority of these descendants still live within a day's drive of the home farm, and many much closer than that.

My grandpa, Vince Bier, was the oldest of the Four Bier Boys. He worked as a field manager for Libby's and bought 80 acres a few miles from the home farm. Gene Bier bought the land just adjacent to the home farm. Alfie Bier, the youngest, never left the home farm and eventually took over its operation. Ed Bier, the second eldest, left his agrarian roots—reluctantly, some say—to join the Bier family tradition of priesthood. He reportedly missed the farm, though, along with his brothers, nieces, and nephews.

Some say he'd have preferred to follow his true passion—football. Ed was a talented football player. Legend had it that he would much rather have played football for Notre Dame than matriculate at the seminary. However, his mother promised Ed's life to God in exchange for saving it after he injured himself as preschooler falling out of a tree. The degree that this bargain influenced the path of Father Ed's life isn't really clear. But the story is accepted lore among the descendants of The Four Bier Boys. In the end, his parents' wishes for him won out, and the seminary it was.

My family never spent much time with my dad's uncle, Father Ed. He would have been busy with various ecclesiastical pursuits during my childhood. Despite any initial misgivings about his vocation, Father Ed became quite a mover and shaker in the Roman Catholic Diocese of Madison, Wisconsin. My grandmother's files burst with clippings, testimonials, and mass cards about her brother-in-law. So, while I didn't know him in life, I still knew him in the same way that genealogists come to know any number of long-since-dead relatives.

In 1951, after completing seminary, Father Ed's religious career was launched with an elaborate first mass at the Bier family home parish: St. Mary's in Janesville, Wisconsin. The Biers were some of the original parishioners of this church, created to tend to the spiritual needs of the numerous German immigrants in the area. The parish archives are littered with the baptisms, weddings, and funerals of hundreds of Biers. There were a few celebratory first masses, too, including Father Ed's. Newspaper accounts of the event noted that it was attended by 12 cousins who entered the religious life, five priests and seven nuns. In the German tradition, several younger cousins also participated, appearing in a mock wedding meant to symbolize Father Ed's "marriage" to a religious life. A photo shows him standing solemnly, clad in sumptuous vestments, between his beaming parents, first-generation Americans, living the Catholic dream. Following this ceremonial debut, he occupied parish positions across southern Wisconsin. In addition to duties typical to a parish priest, he assumed additional leadership roles. From an undated obituary,

Active in civic life, [Monsignor Bier] is remembered especially as an advocate of the ecumenical efforts of the church gaining many friends in the Ecumenical television broadcasts in the 1960's over Channel 3. Many were the day-by-day, month-by-month, year-by-year extracurricular responsibilities that were his. Representing the entire State of Wisconsin, he was responsible for the review of the work of the State Legislature for the entire Provincial Conference beginning in 1978 until his recent illness. Diocesan Consultor, Dean of the Madison Deanery, President of the Madison Priests Senate, member of the newly formed Priests Council, are just a few of these responsibilities. In February of 1967, his outstanding zeal and untiring sacrifice were acknowledged by Pope Paul VI, being given the title of Monsignor.

To say that the figure of Father Ed loomed large is an understatement. In those days, German Catholic parents prayed for at least one child's entrance into religious life. When Father Ed was elevated to the title of Monsignor, his stock within the family rose to untouchable levels. Despite this, whenever he was back on the home farm, he was just one of The Four Bier Boys. He always blended seamlessly into the chaotic, competitive atmosphere at the Bier family.

I have only two memories of him. The first was a brief visit when I was around nine, during which he gifted my then-infant brother a long metal fire truck, complete with ladders that raised and lowered and a hose that unspooled. Neither I nor my two sisters were recognized in such a way by Father Ed. That he paid special recognition to his nephew's first-born son wasn't particularly surprising. My father was an avid amateur athlete, and after three daughters, a son was a long-awaited partner in the sporting life. Father Ed shared a similar disposition.

My second memory of Father Ed is visiting his home near Madison after he was diagnosed with cancer. He was jaundiced and tinged a sickly bright yellow. The time between his diagnosis and death passed quickly. Ed was the second of The Four Bier Boys to die; his younger brother, Gene, also succumbed to cancer ten years earlier. When the two surviving brothers, Vince and Alfie, went to the reading of Ed's will, they were shocked. Five days before he died—while he was a bedridden hospice patient—his will was changed. Everything that would have gone to the church and his brothers now went to his long-serving, universally mistrusted housekeeper. She was an unpleasant, older-middle aged woman who was with him for many years—the opposite of Ginny. She didn't even let his brothers take the shotgun that Ed used as a boy. It was not a good time. My grandpa, Vince, wanted to challenge the will in court, but Alfie talked him out of it. Did they really want to know what all might be revealed, were they to kick over the rock that was Ed and the housekeeper's relationship? In the end, they set their jaws and grimly accepted the loss of any of their brother's heirlooms.

Other than this despised housekeeper, I was unaware of any indication that Father Ed may have had a relationship with a woman. There were rumors of a crisis of faith that brought him home from the seminary for a time prior to his ordination. By all accounts, once the crisis passed, he pursued his work with focus and good humor, never looking back to life on the farm.

So, when I read Liz's email intimating that Father Ed may have been Kathleen's father, I bridled.

From: Me
To: Liz
CC: Kathleen LeFranc

OMG, that is just awful. I have never heard this—Father Ed Bier is my father's uncle and this would be earth shattering. He is very much a beloved figure. Just to make sure, are we talking Father Ed that became a Monsignor? Son of Edward Bier?

AB

I worried about what such a revelation would do to the Biers in general, and my own father in particular. He and my mother are, to put it mildly, big into being Catholic. I can count on one hand the number of Sundays that they've missed mass. My mother keeps a small bottle of emergency holy water in her purse, for pity's sake. I naively assumed that Dad couldn't handle a simultaneous blow to both his family's integrity and his Church. So, I didn't mention Liz's letter to him.

Instead, I called my mom. She was gobsmacked. Her impressions of Father Ed were the same as mine. And furthermore, she never picked up on any whispered secrets surrounding him. If *she* hadn't heard any murmurings, there simply weren't any there to begin with. At that point, I'd done all that I was willing to do to investigate the preposterous claim. As I awaited replies from Kathleen's newfound cousin and fellow sleuth, Liz, I resolved that I wouldn't be able to assist them any further.

From: Liz
To: Me
CC: Kathleen LeFranc

Yes, the Fr. Ed who became Msgr. That's why we're trying to be really careful. The priest brought Virginia down to Illinois and he visited her regularly during her pregnancy. This Illinois family knew that the priest was the father of the baby. They said it was "evident." And we think he had something to do with St. Mary's church, where Fr. Ed worked.

Kathleen shows a "Dennis Parr" as a second or third cousin in her DNA relatives list and he does not appear at all on my DNA relative list. We know DNA can be funny, but we wondered if Kathleen could be a double "Bier" (both sides) which might explain Dennis Parr (Parrs being related to Biers) being shown as her 2nd/3rd cousin and not mine.

We have worked on this for many months — collecting info and articles and talking to other people — and pinpointing memories —and eliminating and digging — hard to put it all into this email, but maybe Kathleen can explain better. We both concluded separately that we think we have it narrowed down.

Liz

[DNA is, in fact, quite funny, but not quite for the reasons that Liz suggests. However, she was correct that any relatives belonging to Kathleen and not to Liz were from her father's side of the family.]

Since I already decided to step away from the mystery, I didn't bother to pick apart Liz's email. However, I knew immediately that locating a potential priest in the Bier family tree wasn't as simple a task as she suggested. In most families, if you asked for a priest, he was easy to identify. In sprawling, rural, German-Catholic mess of the Biers, there were at least five that I knew off the top of my head.

The suggested paternal link to the Biers was through a distant cousin of the last name Parr. There may have been more potential priests than even those five in that huge mess of a tree. I couldn't begin to ascertain why Liz immediately settled on Father Ed. I attempted to remain calm and impassive, a trait for which I'm not particularly well known, and sent off a reply.

From: Me
To: Liz
Cc: Kathleen LeFranc

Hi Liz,

I've been thinking about your email all day. I am not going to be able to help by directly questioning any of my Bier relatives on the possibility of Fr. Ed having a child. My reasons for deciding this are threefold. First, the evidence for paternity is, at this point, circumstantial at best. Keep in mind that there were at least five other Bier cousins in Fr. Ed's generation at that time that would have had the same degree of relation to Dennis Parr that were priests. Secondly, as far as I know, Fr. Ed was never assigned to a St. Mary's. Finally, in terms of my family, news such as this would only do harm, especially at this particular time of grief at the loss of a loved one. There are still living family members of Fr. Ed's generation alive, and a revelation such as this would be particularly crushing right now; it would not, I predict, be greeted with the open-armed welcome that Kathleen would hope for.

Certainly, if at some point, facts become clearer, time passes, and situations change, my feelings may alter. Right now, however, I don't think I'll be able to be of assistance on this hunt. While I feel for Kathleen, I naturally feel more of an obligation to safeguard the well-being of my immediate family members.

I hope that we can continue to correspond on other issues, and I will certainly be interested in the outcome of the search, regardless of what it may be.

Angie

From: Liz
To: Me
Cc: Kathleen LeFranc

Angie - I agree with you. We were only asking if you ever heard anything.

For my part, there is no big agenda. Just curiosity and a search that does no harm! Otherwise, what does it all accomplish at this point, right?!

Just FYI – the *Janesville Daily Gazette* on 5/24/57 lists Fr. Edward Bier as Assistant Pastor at St. Mary's.

And this, from Kathleen: "Well when I met Dennis Parr's sister at St. Mary's in Janesville, she mentioned that everything in the Bier family, the Parr family and I believe the Roethle family seems to all center around St. Mary's. There is a big article in the paper about Father Ed's ordination and the big procession was at St. Mary's. Everyone was there. The Biers, the Parrs, the Roethles. My mother was in the procession when she was 14 at the time."

This is neither here nor there.... just know that there was lots of miscellaneous data that directed us to a certain point. I'm not going to push for anything. No problem. It's a pursuit that hopefully does no more harm than what has already happened.

Angie - all of this started because I was curious about what a DNA test (Ancestry.com and 23 and Me) would show me!!!! Quite a surprise –!

Have a good day - not too far down the road is a wonderful Wisconsin fall...

Liz

The article she mentioned in the Janesville *Daily Gazette* is actually about the celebratory first mass of another Janesville priest. Father Ed and others are listed as assistants for the occasion, not permanent fixtures at the church. Traditionally, a newly minted priest celebrates their first official mass at their natal parish and invites any friends, relatives and colleagues to help him with the service, whether they have any connection to the church itself or not. This was a slight misreading on Liz's part.

What she said about St. Mary's in Janesville is true. It was established by the emigrant German Catholic community—of which all of the named families were a part. I grew up in that parish and attended the school through eighth grade, as did scores of Biers.

Having made my point, I should have left well enough alone. In addition to being scrupulously organized, however, I have a painful need for the last word. I couldn't resist one final email.

From: Me
To: Liz
Cc: Kathleen LeFranc

Thanks for following up. I probably read too much into what you were asking of me.

Just because I'm a stickler for details, as far as I know, Fr. Ed was only <u>ordained</u> at St. Mary's. He never served there...
St. Mary's Janesville was and is very much the home parish of the Valentine Bier family, and really all of the Bier family priests were ordained there.

I'm looking forward to fall indeed!

Angie

Through all of this exchange, the woman at the center of it all, Kathleen, remained silent, allowing Liz to communicate on her behalf. She eventually wrote to me.

From: Kathleen LeFranc
To: Me

Dear Angie,

Thank you so much for responding. I loved following your blog. It seemed like an amazing trip to follow the family lineage.
I live in Southern California, but I grew up in Chicago with an amazing family surrounding me. Finding DNA relatives, even at my age (I turn 65 in October), is rather overwhelming.

Here is a quick version of my backstory. I was adopted when I was two weeks old. When I started to ask questions about my birth family as an adult, my parents told me what they knew. A couple of years ago, I searched for my mother, but all the records were lies, so I had the State of Illinois search for me. They also couldn't find anything and suggested that I do DNA testing which is how I found family on both Roethle and Bier sides.

I came to Wisconsin a couple years ago to meet one of my cousins, Barb Surwillo, whose grandfather was a Roethle. She took me to our great grandfather's farm and gave me a beautiful tour. She gave me the family trees and has been very helpful.

I would love to find out who my father is, but not in any way that would hurt anybody. I know that people in the family know about this because it appears my mother was not a very quiet person. According to Liz, she came back to Wisconsin and had a bit of a drinking problem and caused quite a stir now and then. Liz even knew that she had given up the baby.

Anyway, I'm excited to meet new family members and learn more about my "origin story".

I do not want to put anyone out or make anyone feel uncomfortable in anyway.

I sure hope you understand. Again, thank you so much for responding.

Kathleen McHugh LeFranc

Most of what she shared was a rehashing of Liz's notes. However, in retrospect, Kathleen's tone was conciliatory and calm. Perhaps if I received Kathleen's note first, I might have been more immediately receptive. Perhaps if I knew her better, I might have been more forthcoming. At that moment, though, I was feeling only two things: protective and right. I decided that Liz and Kathleen's understanding of the facts of the Bier genealogy and genetics was muddled. And, furthermore, not my problem. I filed the email chain away and tried not to think about it anymore.

Fat chance.

The Four Bier Boys: Gene, Vince, Alfie, and Ed

Father Ed's first mass. His cousin serves as "bride."

Father Ed in later years

Chapter Three
Snowbound

Summer turned into fall, and my family of four settled back into the school year routine. Despite leaving the medical profession three years earlier, my days remained full. I made sure to keep them that way, and dedicated Thursday afternoons to catching up with genealogy. I still had huge bins of artifacts in my office that never seemed to diminish, and most Thursdays, I spent time sorting through the papers and ephemera. I also blogged on genealogy, including updates from our new friends in Ketzelsdorf. I corresponded with Biers who were relocated from Ketzelsdorf to other areas of Germany after WWII. Finally, I learned a startling fact—the name Bier likely derived from the Old German word for "bear" rather than for "beer!"

And despite having officially "signed off," I did a bit of sleuthing into the Kathleen mystery. I checked up on Father Ed's whereabouts around the time of her birth. I shared the string of emails from Liz and Kathleen with my sister, who knew even more about genetics than I did. She confirmed that the conclusions being drawn from a 23andme report were a stretch and based on a few wrong assumptions. So, I reassured myself...but I still wondered. And I still nosily wished that I was somehow still involved.

I got a lot done over that fall and winter. It was with a feeling of accomplishment that I helped my husband load the two kids and dog into the SUV for spring break. For this trip, we wanted a destination within a reasonable day's drive from home. Since no April warmth could be found within an easy drive of our Milwaukee suburb, we skipped warmth altogether and headed north. Door County, Wisconsin, was a summertime favorite for our crew. We hoped that the springtime version of our happy place would prove worthwhile. I was dozing in the passenger seat somewhere into the four-hour drive when my phone startled me awake. I picked it up and saw that my dad was calling. He is not one to just call for a chat, so I forced myself awake to answer.

"Hey, Ang," he greeted me. "Say, so my cousin, Jan, called the other day. You remember her, you talked to her about genealogy? She was Mom's O.B. nurse?"

Sure, I remembered her. She was listed on my genealogy contact list as a member of a branch of the southern Wisconsin Bier clan. True to form, my dad had multiple ways of knowing her, not merely their second-cousin relatedness. Dad lived in his hometown for all but two years of his life, when he finished his undergraduate degree in Madison. I suspect the time away nearly killed him—he relished familiarity and routine. He liked knowing every other person that he ran into around town. So, while he was related to Nurse Jan, he also crossed paths with her in day to day life. And she assisted at my delivery. No big deal. Jan didn't have any of her own children, so we spoke in the past about my inheriting some of her family heirlooms someday.

"Yeah, I remember her. What's up?" I said.

"She's been talking to a woman who was adopted and thinks that her dad may have been Father Ed." That thud would be the sound of my jaw hitting the floor. I recovered and noted that Dad's voice was very matter-of-fact, not overwrought.

"Yeah, I emailed with that woman myself awhile back, but didn't think there was anything to it," I said.

"Well, I can't see it either, but I told Jan she might want to give you a call, cuz you know the most about the genealogy and that."

"Sure, I'll give her a call. You know, I didn't want to get involved initially. I didn't want to shake anyone up, especially Auntie Eleanor." Eleanor was the lone survivor of the Four Bier Boys' generation. She was the youngest, Alfie's, wife, still living at the home farm. "I figured that, Father Ed being her brother-in-law and all, she'd be the one to know anything if there was anything to know. What do you think about trying to ask her?"

"I already did. The other day, when we stopped by after church to take her communion, Ma and I asked. Eleanor said that, no, she'd never heard any inkling of such a thing."

I couldn't believe that he dared to bring up something like that to his elderly aunt! Then again, he certainly knew her temperament far better than I did.

"What'd she say? Was she appalled?"

"No, no. But she thought it was pretty much impossible."

"I'm glad she wasn't irritated or offended," I said.

"No, she wasn't. Actually, she didn't seem to think his being a priest was the thing that made the situation unlikely. Father Ed and the woman, Ginny Roethle, were actually cousins, and he'd never have something to do with his cousin."

"Well, it's an interesting question. I'll get ahold of Jan and maybe I'll see if I can get back in touch with the woman. Her name's Kathleen, by the way."

And with that, we signed off and my hamster wheel mind began to whir. I was sitting in the passenger seat of the car with no access to my laptop and genealogy files. I grabbed a receipt and a pencil and tried to sketch out a family tree from memory. How exactly were Father Ed and Ginny related? By extension, how exactly were Kathleen and I related? It all had to do with another German family that settled in Southern Wisconsin. This one was called the Roethles. They were from a completely different area of Europe than the Bohemian German Biers and their expatriate community in Janesville. Almost 50 years before the Biers arrived, the Roethle progenitors emigrated from the Black Forest region of Germany and set up shop in a small town about 60 miles from where the Biers lived. They arrived with more resources and became successful, prosperous farmers fairly quickly. About the only things that the Roethles held in common with the Biers was the German language and a strict adherence to Catholicism.

John and Katherine Roethle had a family of eight kids. Two of these kids married Biers. One of them, Rosalia, married Edward Bier, and became the mother of The Four Bier Boys, including Father Ed and my own grandfather. After Rosalia made that connection to Edward, her brother, Leo, was introduced to the Bier family. He ended up marrying Edward's niece, Helen Bier. Edward was around the same age as his niece, Helen. Long story short, two Roethle siblings married a Bier uncle / niece combination.

So, Leo Roethle was Father Ed's uncle, on his mom's side. Leo's daughter, Ginny, was his first cousin. Easy enough. But just to make things more confusing, Ed was also related to Ginny through his father. On his dad's side, Ginny was Ed's first cousin once removed. Father Ed Bier and Ginny Roethle were both first cousins and first cousins once removed. The preceding confusion is why many throw up their hands in annoyance and frustration when we genealogists get going. Me? I was hot on the case and started outlining detailed notes on the back of the piece of scrap paper. I didn't notice any of the scenery as we drove further and further north, the sky growing darker and heaped with clouds.

* * *

By the time we finished unpacking at the vacation cottage, the wind shifted. By the following morning, the blizzard began. Over the next two days, Door County received record-breaking snow and we were housebound. Luckily, we had plenty of food and entertainment, puzzles and games. The house had a Netflix account and our daughters were bingeing on a television series. My husband and I watched peripherally and hung out on our laptops. He indulged in sports and video games. I was up to my eyeballs in what I came to call The Kathleen Mystery.

I guess I never really gave up on the mystery after all. After terminating my email contact with Liz and Kathleen the previous summer, I stewed over the question and concluded that it simply *couldn't* be Father Ed. It seemed like my role in solving the mystery of Kathleen's paternity was complete. Out of sight, out of mind. But then—the mystery essentially came knocking at my door! And the people I was worried about upsetting—weren't. Maybe I could play a useful role after all? I dove back into the fray and sent off an email to Kathleen and her sidekick, Liz.

From: Me
To: Kathleen LeFranc, Liz

Hi, ladies!

I heard through the Janesville grapevine that you are continuing your quest to identify your birth father, Kathleen. I wanted to let you know that I did some questioning of women in the family—we are generally privy to secrets, I've found—and I can't find a speck of family lore that has Fr. Ed fathering a child. Kathleen—I think you called Jan in Janesville, who then called my dad to ask if he knew anything, which is how word got back to me. My dad did the thing that I'd been too chicken to do and asked the last member of that generation still alive, Fr. Ed's sister-in-law, Eleanor, and she had no suspicions at all. Also, interestingly, no one seemed particularly appalled by the notion of Fr. Ed having a child, rather they were really hesitant about the idea that he'd have a child with his own cousin.

So, at this point, I don't have any agenda other than trying to figure this mystery out. I have to admit it—I haven't stopped thinking about it and I'm a sucker for a mystery. If I remember correctly, your main paternity clues were:

1. Family and friends reporting that Virginia had a relationship with a priest. This seems pretty much an established fact.

2. A genetic connection to a Bier—I can't remember the details on this. This is the tricky bit. My sister is a genetic counselor and I'm a physician by training, and we're wondering if this connection could exist due to the fact that Virginia was related to the Biers in her own right, given that her grandmother was actually a Bier. I'm doing this from memory on spring break, sorry for the lack of detail. This could be a red herring in terms of looking for the priest among the immediate Bier clan. If we do think there's an additional genetic tie to

the Biers outside of Virginia's ancestors, there are at least half a dozen other Bier priests that fit the timing.

3. A report that Virginia stayed at a St. Mary's church—I think. Again, Fr. Ed never worked at a St. Mary's. St. Mary's Janesville was the parish where he grew up and his parents attended, he said masses there, but he never lived or worked there.

Do you have any more details as to which parish the priest was at? Could you request parish employment records?

I'm not sure if this is helpful or merely annoying, but I especially want to share the lack of any family lore, and the trickiness of interpreting genetic data in the Bier/Roethle situation.

Angie

I reviewed my draft before sending it off, checking for tone and clarity. After hitting send, I had a hard time concentrating on the TV and board games. Kathleen's paternity seemed eminently solvable! I hoped that they'd still let me in on the sleuthing. Like a Skinner rat with a snack box, I repeatedly refreshed my inbox. As my youngest daughter and I won a game of euchre, I was rewarded with a new message. I suggested that we take a brief break from cards and curled up on the cushy chair that I staked out for the duration of so-called spring break.

From: Liz
To: Me, Kathleen LeFranc

Angela,
I'm so delighted to hear from you! I'm sure you'll hear from Kathleen separately, she lives in California, I live in Florida. Kathleen has so much more information than I do.
First of all, thank you to you and your family for the help you have given by asking the questions.

Kathleen has been seeing DNA matches to Dennis Parr (from the Frank Bier line) and I show no DNA connection to him. I know that DNA is a mix and hodgepodge and that siblings can even be different DNA mixes. So, I'm just setting that aside for now.

An unnamed priest brought pregnant Virginia (Ginny) from Wisconsin to Evanston, Illinois, to a family named Brummel, where she lived and helped with housework and helped with their little children during her pregnancy. A now-grown daughter of the Brummels spoke with Kathleen and informed her that they, too, knew that the priest that brought Virginia to their house and visited her weekly throughout the pregnancy was actually the baby's father.

Kathleen has information that the Roethles, Biers, and Parrs attended church at St. Mary's in Janesville, which they considered the main church. It was understood that Virginia was doing housekeeping for a priest somewhere in some parish. She also wanted to keep the baby, but notes state that her mother wouldn't allow it.

There are so many aspects of this situation that make it difficult for researching it ...hopefully, Kathleen can fill in other information that she has — and why we approached you in the first place. . ..

Again - thank you ~ Attached is a photo of Kathleen.

Liz

Wow, there were so many things to unpack here. Liz mentioned a DNA connection to yet another Ketzelsdorf-to-Wisconsin family, the Parrs. Childbearing was a popular hobby in this Bohemian German family on a scale surpassing that of even the Biers. Southern Wisconsin Parrs were a dime a dozen. It was common knowledge that there was some connection between the two families, but I never teased it out completely. Liz suggested that the connection lay somewhere in the Frank Bier family line. I'd have to check on that. Frank was one of the Valentine Ten. He was one that I didn't know so well, save for the fact that photos captured his simply amazing cheekbones. Over the years, people would occasionally ask if I knew how the Biers and the Parrs were related, but I never had time to tease the relationship out.

"The Valentine Ten" was my shorthand for the ten children that begat the dynasty of Wisconsin Biers. Valentine Bier's family left Ketzelsdorf, Bohemia, and settled in Wisconsin in 1882. After years of struggle and with the help of their ten children, they eventually clawed their way out of poverty and founded a successful farm. This farm just outside of Janesville was a center of industry during the day. At night, it was a center of socialization for the expatriate Bohemian German community. Bier family diaries complete each day's entry with an enumeration of the "visitors of the evening." On Sundays, those visitors might number to 20 or 30. They played cards, sang German songs, and drank beer. These visitors often included members of the Parr family.

Eventually, my great-grandfather, Edward, the youngest of the Valentine Ten, inherited the home farm and it continued to serve as a hub of socialization. Then, after Edward retired, the youngest of The Four Bier Boys, Alfie, took over the farm. At present, Alfie's widow, Eleanor, remains ensconced in the family home and continues to entertain visitors; my own parents see her every Sunday when they stop by to take her communion. One of Alfie's and Eleanor's sons turned the former pig barn into a Man Cave and hosts card games there. So, from Valentine on down, a truth has held for the Bier family: hard work is good, socialization is even better. Liz suggested that, not only had the Parrs and the Biers socialized together, but that a Parr connection existed with one of the Valentine Ten. This was news to me.

As Liz said, there were many aspects that made this mystery difficult to research, but there were so many leads as well! Kathleen lived in California and Liz in Florida, but I lived smack in the heart of the places involved. I was convinced that my boots on the ground were going to be invaluable.

My boots, my archives, and my basic knowledge of genetics. I pulled together my notes on the back of receipts, the emails, and my archives. I started to get organized, treating this like the solvable mystery that it was.

Casebook summary
<u>FACTS</u>
•Kathleen's mother was Virginia (Ginny) Roethle
<u>QUESTIONS</u>
•Does Kathleen actually want me involved?

St. Mary's church, Janesville, Wisconsin, was founded by expatriate German Bohemians, including the Biers.

The Valentine & Katherine Bier family, featuring the Valentine Ten. My great-grandfather is in the bottom right corner. The eldest brother, John, is just to his left. They were born 20 years apart. The tiny, elderly woman in the center is Katherine (Jiru) Bier's mother. She is often the only smiling face in family portraits. All of the unmarried daughters continue to wear white. Back row: Caroline Bier, Anna (Sister Veronica) Bier, Amalia (Bier) Bott, Johanna Jiru, Father Charles Bier, Frank Bier, Louis Bier. Front row: Emily (Bier) Gassert, Frances (Bier) Hanauska, Katherine (Jiru) Bier, Valentine Bier, John Bier, Edward Bier.

The Valentine Bier home farm, taken sometime in the 1980's. Several of the outbuildings, including the barn, have since collapsed or been razed.

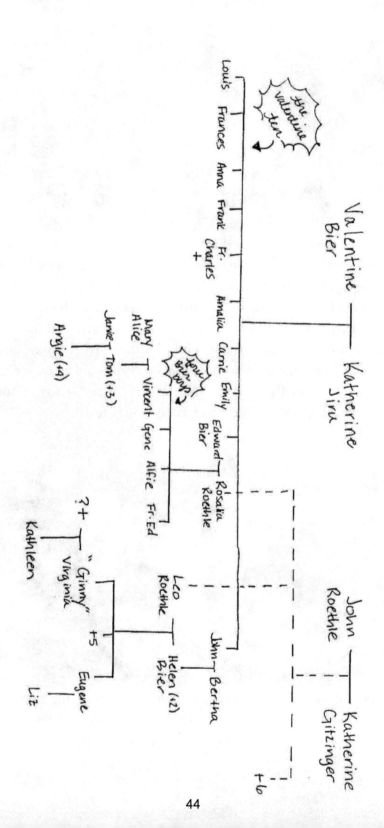

Chapter Four
A Scholarly Approach

While the snow continued to fall in northern Wisconsin, I hunkered down in my overstuffed chair and thanked my lucky stars for the time I took to digitize my archives. I could do almost as much research from there, under a blanket, as I could at my home office. The emails flew fast and furious between Liz, Kathleen and me. I sifted through correspondence and highlighted what seemed to be established fact. I then added in my own supplementary facts and included the questions that were bubbling up in my mind. I sent off the document.

From: Me
To: Kathleen LeFranc, Liz

Ladies—
Because I can't help myself, I made a summary document of the facts of Kathleen's paternity as I understand them. . . . See what you think.
AB

FACTS
•Virginia Roethle was sent to the convent and at some point, she wanted to leave; she was sent to live at and keep house for a rectory.
•Virginia was 19 when she became pregnant, presumably while keeping house for the priest(s).
oGinny was forbidden by her mother to keep the baby or to return home in her condition. The family kept the pregnancy a fairly guarded secret.
oDNA testing and family history confirm Ginny's baby is Kathleen.
•A priest "uncle," likely father of the baby, arranged with Father Paul McArdle to have Virginia taken care of during pregnancy.
oFr. McArdle was a priest at St. Mary's, Evanston [Illinois].

oShe was sent to live with the Brummels, parishioners of Father McArdle, during her pregnancy.

•The person who dropped her off and her sole visitor during her pregnancy was a priest; the host family "knew" that he was the father of the baby. Liz's family "knew" that the father of Aunt Ginny's baby was a priest.

•Kathleen was born October 15, 1952.

oSham names on her birth certificate: Mother: Elizabeth Louise Becker Father: Jerome Leo Rohner

•The McHughs privately adopted Kathleen at 2 weeks of age and she grew up in Chicago.

oThe McHughs are first cousins to Fr. McArdle

oDNA testing confirms <u>no</u> biologic relation between Kathleen and either the McHughs or McArdles.

•Kathleen is related to a Dennis Parr

o23andMe shows them to be "third cousins".

oLiz Mueller, Kathleen's maternal first cousin, is NOT similarly related to Dennis Parr.

o Therefore, Kathleen's father must be related to Dennis Parr.

•For awhile, Kathleen has wondered if Father Ed Bier could be her father, because she understood that Dennis Parr and Ed Bier are both descendants of Valentine Bier.

▪No one in the Edward Bier family has any inkling that Father Ed fathered a child, including his sister-in-law who was married into the family by 1952.

▪He was 30 years old at the time that Kathleen was conceived.

▪Virginia was his first cousin.

QUESTIONS

•How did Liz's family "know" that Virginia got pregnant by a priest?

•How did the pregnancy host family "know" that the priest was the father of the baby?

•The person who visited her was reportedly a priest, an uncle, and the father of the baby

oDo we believe any of these to be true? In other words, are we assuming that he wasn't really an uncle either?

•How old did the priest that escorted Virginia appear to be? Are there any family members of the host family alive today that would recognize a picture?

•What is Father McArdle's professional resume? Where did he go to school?

oThe father/priest was likely a school or work colleague of his

•Can we confirm where Virginia was sent to the convent and then to keep house?

•Can I see actual language from 23andMe regarding the degree of relation between Kathleen and Dennis Parr? The phrase "third cousins" can mean any number of things.

•Are there other priests in the Parr tree???

Of all of the purported facts, the one on which I was most hung up, was that Kathleen's father was a priest. This assertion seemingly drove Kathleen and Liz's search thus far. I needed to confirm it. After all, if this tidbit was merely conjecture, we were barking up the wrong tree entirely. A priest-father was based wholly on the recollections of a few people. First, Liz said that her family "knew" that Ginny got pregnant with a priest's child. I wanted some more evidence for this . . . did Ginny herself report it to her siblings, nieces, and nephews? Or had it been familial conjecture based on the fact that she'd been living with a bunch of priests at the time? Or had Liz merely created this memory in light of the information that Kathleen supplied?

The other source for the priest-father fact was the Brummels, Ginny's host family during her pregnancy. They reported that Ginny's lone visitor was a priest, and that this priest was obviously her lover. This mysterious man was described as three things: a priest, her uncle, and her lover. Which were true? I trusted that he was, in fact, a priest. If a man wanted to remain anonymous, why would he don clerical garb for his surreptitious visits? Priest was not a good disguise for someone wishing to remain incognito.

I believed that her visitor really was a priest. But was he really her lover, the father of her baby? What about his behavior made it so clear that he was a lover and not a benignly caretaking uncle? What if the

Brummels' interpretations of the priest's care for Ginny was wrong, and his affection was purely uncle-ly? What if this priest really *was* her uncle, as he reported? Did she have an uncle in the clergy who was simply helping his niece hide an unplanned pregnancy? Or, could he have been covering for Ginny's lover, someone that he knew or was related to?

At least one of the three descriptors must have been a lie. Priest, uncle, lover. Which one to strike? I really wasn't prepared to contemplate a mystery in which the same man was all three.

I hoped that Kathleen or Liz would answer my questions about the man's identity as interpreted by the Brummels. Alas, Kathleen focused more on my questions about the genetic testing results. In her mind, the matter of her father's being a priest was settled history and not a hot topic for discussion. Email prevented her from seeing how earnestly I needed to know the answer to that question. No matter, I was pleased to be privy to any answers at that point.

From: Kathleen LeFranc
To: Me

Wow! I am so impressed at how thorough you are. . . I would really suggest, with all your research, you have your DNA tested. I think it will open up vast amounts of information. For me, I have now acquired over 1000 relatives, when my whole life, I thought I was a one and only :). I feel very privileged to have you interested in my search.

PS If you would like explore my 23andme account, let me know. I will give you my access information.

Huzzah! She was happy to have me involved. I was thrilled, and I figured it was time to reveal my hand and let Kathleen know just how much thought I already devoted to her search, and how invested I truly was. Wow, that happened quickly. But if Kathleen was willing to share her genetic information with me, I was willing to jump all-in too.

From: Me
To: Kathleen LeFranc

That would be great! My sister, the geneticist, and I were just on the phone and she's all set to start doing calculations...She's so funny. She says she feels like we need a police-style bulletin board with strings connecting things. She said she's going to stop waxing her lip to develop a cop-like mustache LOL :)

AB

Ah, yes, my sister, Louise. Out of my four siblings, I've always been closest to Louise. We enjoyed the same things, such as cooking, reading, musical theatre and obsessively watching the Olympics. The introvert to my extrovert, we were each other's sounding board in many matters. The previous summer, she confirmed my confusion over some of the statements that the two women made about their DNA reports. Of course, as soon as I'd rejoined the case, I kept her apprised of the development.

I trusted her opinion. Louise is a genetic counselor, a professional trained to help patients navigate the pitfalls of genetic testing for diseases and conditions. In addition to this qualification, she spent several years working at Chicago's Lincoln Park Zoo, managing a national database of zoo populations with an eye on maintaining genetic diversity across breeding stock. This pedigree made her uniquely suited to mull over questions of genetic testing and relatedness over multiple generations. Plus, she was funny. And she was on the case.

Casebook summary

FACTS

• Kathleen is related to Liz through her mother, Ginny Roethle

•Kathleen is related to Dennis Parr whereas Liz is not related to him. Presumably, then, Kathleen is related to Dennis Parr through her father; her father is somewhere in Dennis Parr's tree.

QUESTIONS

•How certain are we that the priest visitor was Ginny's lover, not her uncle as reported?

•Does Ginny have any living relatives who might know where she was living when she became pregnant with Kathleen?

•Is there any significance to the sham names on Kathleen's birth certificate?

•Can we use the information in Kathleen's 23andme report to narrow down who her father might be?

•What of the Parrs?

Chapter Five
Watson, Crick, 23, and Me

Louise is a busy, busy woman. However, she was intrigued and responded quickly to my questions.

From: Louise Bier
To: Me
I'm going to have to do more research on exactly what 23andme is looking at. . . .. There is a snippet in their comparison tool that shows Parr & Liz Mueller share a small region of SNPs, although I really don't know enough to interpret that. Maybe everyone would share some amount of SNPs on that? I don't know. Don't jump to any conclusions. I can't believe she shared her password with us! There is actual clinical grade information in there!

Seriously. There was just too much. I called her. "Can you believe it?" I asked, launching right into things, as sisterly sisters do.

"Um, no," Louise replied. "I can't believe she's just letting us go through all of this!"

"I know, right? Honestly, Louise, she seems like a real straight-shooter. You know how we were put off by some of the early emails from Liz?"

"Yeah, for good reason. She was way off base..."

"Right. Well, Kathleen is much more measured and on-board about taking our time and sorting everything out before jumping to conclusions. So, what are you thinking?"

"What I'm thinking is that this is going to be a bigger puzzle than we can solve in one sitting, or just over the phone, From what you've told me, there's a fair amount of intermarriage and multiple-relatedness in the involved families, right?"

"Right. I can't even describe it in words. You need visual aids," I confirmed, glancing at my hand-drawn trees.

"And the nearest relative that gives a clue to paternity is a Parr, right?"

"Right. And I'm not even sure how we're related to the Parrs at all," I said. "I just know there's a ton of them around Janesville, just like the Biers, and that people are always saying we're related somehow, but I've never been able to figure it out."

"Hmmm. Well, I think you need to focus on sorting that bit out," she said. "I'll see if I can spend a little time with the genetic results and come up with a plan or algorithm to try and assign likely paternal lines to the results."

"Do you know much about 23andme?" I asked.

"Mostly what I've read or heard at conferences. I never considered submitting my own sample, I'm not totally comfortable with their open-ended privacy policies, and using submitted samples for research. I've already had my genome analyzed through our NIH project anyway," Louise said.

"Do you think it's a bad idea for everyone?"

"No, not necessarily. I just think I kind of know too much, if that makes any sense."

"Yeah, I can see that," I said pondering. "Gah, I'm just so excited! It seems solvable, right?" I nearly shrieked through the phone.

"Totally. I was thinking that I feel like I'm in some sort of a detective movie right now."

Lucky, nerdy us!

* * *

When Louise's email casually threw out the term "SNPs," I knew that I needed to dust off my genetics knowledge and answer some basic questions. Starting with what, exactly, was 23andme telling us?

At the time that Kathleen first contacted me, 23andme was a full-fledged cultural phenomenon. It was around for over a decade and was the first company to offer direct-to-consumer genetic analysis. Before that, having one's DNA analyzed required medical or laboratory connections. Kathleen joined more than 3 million people and submitted a tube of saliva to the California-based company. In her case, it paid dividends. The results led to her biological mother and provided a starting point for finding her biological father as well.

I logged into Kathleen's 23andme account and looked at her results. When Kathleen reported that she found over 1,000 relatives, she wasn't kidding. I studied the table of thousands. After a few minutes, I figured out the general idea. 23andme took Kathleen's results, compared them to other people's, and generated a list of people to whom she was related. It did so by computing how much DNA she shared with other users. A lot=related. Not much=not related.

But what did "how much DNA" mean? What was 23andme actually comparing? Time to return to some of the big words that Louise mentioned.

The entire human genome, or chain of DNA, consists of over 30,000,000,000 little units known as nucleotides. They are like the individual letters of a massive, multi-volumed book. While it is possible to sort out, or sequence, every single one of these letters, this is rarely done. It's expensive and not particularly useful, for a couple of reasons.

First of all, most of the chain of letters is exactly the same from one person to the next. We are all breathtakingly more similar than we are different. Heck, bonobo monkeys and humans are 99% identical on a DNA level. Humans and bananas are 50% identical on a DNA level. So, if you're trying to sort out how closely two people are related, looking at the whole, redundant chain of DNA is a fool's errand.

The second reason that whole-genome sequencing is rarely done is that there's a lot of filler and nonsense in those 30,000,000,000 nucleotides. Imagine that most of the books are filled with paragraphs' worth of "ummmmmmms."

So, 23andme does not sequence a customer's entire redundant, nonsensical genome. Instead, they target the most telling, variable, clue-rich areas of the 30,000,000,000 and specifically decode only those chunks. These chunks are referred to as SNP's: Single Nucleotide Polymorphisms. "Single nucleotide" means one discrete nucleotide unit, one out of the 30,000,000,000 plus. "Polymorphism" refers to the fact that there's variability between people at that one particular nucleotide unit.

Trust me, just call them SNP's. These SNP's are the rare locations where differences between people can be found. The SNP's are the needles in the whole-genome haystack, and it's those needles that 23andme decodes. About 1,000,000 SNP needles in all! For 23andme, the question "how much DNA do these two people share?" is answered by how many SNP's out of the million checked do two people share.

If Kathleen shared more than a negligible number of SNPs with another 23andme user, that person was flagged as a relative. The program sorted the results so that those with the most shared SNPs were listed first, going down from there. 23andme then took the leap of assigning a relationship status to all of these people. The report listed both the "percent shared" values for each "relative," as well as assigning a relationship name to that person. 100% shared? Identical twin. .01% shared? 23andme would label that person a sixth cousin, someone with whom Kathleen shared a great-great-great-great-great grandparent. Whew. Crazy, heady stuff.

In reality, though, the situation is far more complex than 23andme's lovely table implies. There are actually a number of different ways that two individuals can share a given percentage of DNA. The possibilities increase with more distant relations. For example, 6.25% sharing can happen with: first cousins once removed, half-first cousins, great-great-grandparents/grandchildren, half-uncle or aunt/half niece or nephew, or double-second cousins (16). 23andme automatically identifies 6.25% shared SNPs as first cousins once removed.

That's why relationship information from 23andme can only be used to *verify* a family tree, but never to construct one from the ground up. You still need old-school genealogists and their archives to provide starting points. (This is why Ancestry.com, a 23andme competitor, is so clever. It provides DNA results AND old school family trees in one platform. Smart.)

Kathleen had a list of relatives, all of whom were neatly labeled; but even that wasn't enough to construct a clear family tree and hunt down her biological father. The relationship suggestions were just that—suggestions. Lucky for her, 23andme provided a genealogist relative on her biological mother's side of the family. That's how she found and confirmed Ginny. She stumbled on me another way, and that's how she'd find her father, I hoped.

Traditional genealogists grow trees from firsthand knowledge, documents, and records. We rely on records, which themselves derive from some person's firsthand report. Birth certificates, for example, do not *verify* paternity. Rather, they record for all posterity whatever the mother reported. In Kathleen's case, Ginny Roethle fabricated most, if not all, of the information on that document. When it comes right down to it, birth certificate paternity is, and always has been, a matter of trust.

Nowadays, in addition to the trust-based documents, genealogists have genetics thrown into the mix. There are probably professional symposia that deal with these flummoxes, but I've settled on my own way of reconciling these two worlds. When disagreements crop up between traditional records and genetic data, I embrace them. These conflicts open up fascinating avenues of inquiry. Why might someone give up their child for adoption? Why might a woman lie about the paternity of her child? The data may conflict, but the discrepancies tell a truth in their own right.

* * *

I gave Louise a couple of days before I called her again.

"Hey," I greeted. "Have you had a chance to look at Kathleen's information? And the family trees that I sent?"

"Yeah, there's a lot there. Honestly, Ang, with everything going on here, I feel like we just need some time alone together in a room to work this all out."

"Sorry," I said. I hated to stress people out.

"I mean, I know I can do it. But I just need you here because there are so many questions that I have about the tree that I need you to answer. I wish we just had 48 hours to lock ourselves in a hotel room," she said.

"Well, why don't we?" I asked, wheels turning.

"Why don't we what?"

"Lock ourselves in a hotel room! I'm looking at my calendar; are you free any weekends in August?"

And that's how the great Nashville Genetics Summit of 2018 came to be. We found a weekend, identified the three cheapest nonstop flights out of our respective airports, cross referenced them, and settled on Nashville. We quickly confirmed that Nashville did, in fact, have a Kimpton hotel. Because, come on, 48 hours in a hotel room required a little indulgence.

The game was afoot!

Chapter Six
Growing Up Separate

I saved hundreds of emails between Kathleen and me. So did she. For awhile, our relationship existed in a purely electronic format, germinated from my end during a snowbound spring break. I can't remember when, exactly, all of the details of Kathleen's story fell into place for me, or when our friendship started to take root. We started adding emojis to our notes, eventually signing off with "love" or "xoxo." I do, however, clearly remember the first time that I ever spoke to her.

After exchanging scores of emails, we agreed that it was ridiculous that we hadn't yet spoke. While I am a Generation X-er, I resemble Millennial stereotypes in that I hate talking on the phone. I much prefer texting and listening to voicemail makes my heart race. Needless to say, as the time for our first planned conversation drew near, I was sweaty-palm nervous. I also prefer to have all tricky conversations in the car. These are usually person-to-person encounters, and I find that the confines and inability for either party to escape make for a great venue for Big Talks. Also, it's not awkward to avoid eye contact when one of the parties needs to be driving.

While I wouldn't be speaking to her in person, I planned to carry out my first phone call with Kathleen in my cozy, distraction-free car. I routed the call through my Bluetooth and took notes, all while in the parking lot of my daughters' dance school while they were in ballet class. Kathleen and I first spoke several months into the renewed search, on a shiny, early spring day in late May. April's freak snowstorms were a rapidly-fading (and melting) memory. With my genealogy notebook at my fingers, I nervously called Kathleen. The phone rang once, and I heard it click to life.

"Hello, Cousin!" a friendly voice said, neither too high nor too low. That laughing greeting banished all my worries of awkward silences and painful small talk. Kathleen and I chatted like old friends for the duration of the girls' classes, from stretches to barre work. I filled in the gaps of her story.

Kathleen McHugh was raised in a loving, Irish Catholic family on the west side of Chicago, where she attended mass and Catholic school along with her three siblings. Kathleen always knew she was adopted. Her parents emphasized that she was their "chosen child" and gave her a special book highlighting this. They wove her adoption story, describing a birth mother from a wealthy, political Wisconsin family who wasn't allowed to keep her illegitimate child. That satisfied Kathleen's childish curiosity.

The McHughs were "the best parents and the most wonderful family anyone could hope for." She had one brother who was also adopted, and two younger siblings who were the McHughs' biological offspring. Growing up, she was very close with their parish priest, Father Paul McArdle. Father Paul was also her dad's cousin and arranged her adoption by the McHughs. They went to Notre Dame football games together and had him over for dinner every week. He would someday perform Kathleen's wedding ceremony and baptize her children. As Kathleen grew up, she pieced together the fact that Father Paul carried the secrets of her birth story. However, she never felt like she could ask—nor did she particularly want to.

Kathleen moved to California in 1978 at the age of 26, following her first husband. Despite the distance, she remained close with her family, including Father Paul. The families traded visits back and forth as Kathleen slowly morphed into a California girl. During one of Father Paul's visits they hung out in her jacuzzi under the California sunset. He mused whether Kathleen wanted to ask him any questions about her origin story. Inexplicably, she declined. There was no good reason—she just wasn't ready right then. And so, that was that.

As with so many adoptees, Kathleen's interest in her birth story was piqued when she had her own children. After she gave birth to her son and daughter in 1981 and 1982, she was bothered by questions about the woman who went through those same moments with her. Who was this young Wisconsin girl, who must have experienced the same unconditional, twitterpating love of a mother?

Unfortunately, Father Paul, the man with the answers, died in 1984, and with him any last bits of the truth. Any papers or memoirs that he left were destroyed by the Diocese of Chicago. Oh, to be able to travel back in time to that jacuzzi...

So, she turned to the next logical source: her parents. She asked, and they were sorry to report that Father Paul was the key to it all, and he was gone. They shared what little they knew. In 1951, Father Paul was a newly-minted, associate priest at a church in Evanston, Illinois. One day when the pastor was out, Father Paul received a visit from a priest from Wisconsin. This unnamed priest was there with his "niece" who needed help. The woman was 19, unmarried, and pregnant. Years of searching failed to reveal any link between Father Paul and this mystery priest other than random chance. Perhaps the mystery priest chose Father Paul's church because of its reputation for helping Catholic girls in trouble. The parish was close to The Cradle, a Catholic orphanage; many parishioners took in unwed mothers.

Father Paul handled the situation as the routine matter that it was. He contacted a parish family, the Brummels, who took in unwed mothers in the past, and they agreed to take in this young woman as well. That woman was Ginny, and her baby was Kathleen. This was astonishing news to Kathleen! She actually grew up knowing the Brummels. They attended the same church and socialized with her adoptive family. They knew these intimate facts of Kathleen's birth story for so many years—and never breathed a word.

The only other thing that Kathleen was able to learn from her parents was that all of the information on her birth certificate was false. Perhaps this was because Kathleen's birth and adoption were handled privately. Her ultimate adoption by the McHughs was arranged by Fr. Paul, without the assistance of the orphanage or any other social service agencies. In contrast, most Catholic babies born out of wedlock were adopted through one of several Catholic orphanages in the area—not that these birth certificates were necessarily reliable either.

With those scanty clues in hand, Kathleen gave it the old college try. First, she contacted the Brummels. Kathleen met with several of the remaining family members, including Mrs. Brummel who was, by then, quite elderly. Mrs. Brummel remembered the young woman who was Kathleen's mother; she recalled that her name was Ginny. Kathleen, she said, had her mother's smile. Beyond that, she couldn't offer any details. It was difficult to recall, because the Brummels took in a total of 27 young women over the years. In exchange for discreet housing during their pregnancies, the young women acted as au pairs of sorts for the Brummel family. Mrs. Brummel and her daughter, who was 10 at the time of Kathleen's birth, recalled that Ginny was a pretty young woman, and that her only visitor was a priest. Everyone in the family was simply certain that the priest was Ginny's lover; their behavior together must have been that transparent. Other than that brief sketch, the Brummels knew nothing more.

Kathleen tried to pursue leads from her sham birth certificate. Her father was listed as "Jerome Leo Rohner," so she started researching whether there were priests in Wisconsin by the name of Rohner. She discovered that there had, in fact, been a Father Rohner in Wisconsin in the 1950's. He was in his 60's at the time of her birth, but it was worth a shot. Kathleen contacted his only surviving relative, a niece. The niece was friendly enough and responded to Kathleen, but flatly denied any possibility of her uncle having fathered a child. Kathleen believed her. He had no connections to Ginny's family, he lived in a completely different part of the state, and he was old in 1951. It was a dead end

With no other leads to pursue, Kathleen gave up. She was busy with two young children, too busy to be chasing ghosts.

A few years before contacting me, Kathleen's parents died. She grieved the loss of her beloved parents and, with thoughts of her own mortality and a desire to leave her children a legacy, she resumed her search. This time, she contacted a department within the State of

Illinois who took up research on her behalf. Kathleen ended up working with a very kind woman who investigated her case for 1½ years. Ultimately, this researcher could find nothing either. "Everything in your case file is lies," she told Kathleen. In the 1950s, fabricating information on Catholic adoptees' birth certificates seemed the rule rather than the exception. As a last-ditch effort, the researcher suggested Kathleen submit her DNA to 23andme or Ancestry.com, see if any relatives turned up, and go from there.

And, as Kathleen says, "If it wasn't for Ancestry.com and 23andme, I would've never found my family." In a completely non-spokeswoman way, Kathleen's assertion is true. She sent off her little tube of saliva and within weeks, her results were in. "The spit was it." Suddenly, she was related—actually blood related—to over 1,000 people; she was never blood related to even ONE person ever before! She wasn't separate anymore; she was overwhelmingly connected.

The first relative she made contact with was listed as a second cousin, Barb Surwillo. Lucky for Kathleen, Barb was the historian for her branch of the family, the Roethle family. Barb was a typical oldest child: organized, competent, and bearing a sense of responsibility for her flock. She opened her family tree and her heart to Kathleen immediately, without being absolutely sure of where Kathleen fit in. Kathleen did the logical thing—she flew in from California to Chicago and drove to Wisconsin to meet her cousin. They pored over Barb's extensive family trees and tentatively traced her to Virginia Roethle—Ginny. Barb's trees also helped them to identify a nearest-living relative who might be able to confirm a DNA relationship to Ginny. Ginny had a niece who was also interested in genealogy—Barb's second cousin, Liz. They contacted her.

As soon as Liz saw Kathleen's photo, she knew that she was Ginny's daughter. She had her mother's smile, and much more. In addition to photographic proof, Liz was privy to the family murmurings that Ginny gave up a child for adoption, that she got pregnant by a priest. As far as Liz was concerned, no further evidence was needed. Kathleen learned her lesson, though: the spit was it. So, Liz spat, and the numbers worked, and they knew. Kathleen's birth mother was the young, beautiful, Ginny Roethle.

After identifying Ginny as her mother, Kathleen went back to the Brummels, Ginny's photo in hand. By this time, Mrs. Brummel had died. But her daughter was still alive. It took only a glance. She confirmed that the woman in Liz's photograph was the same Ginny in the yellow dress, the young woman visited by the priest. She again recalled her family whispering about the priest who passed himself off as her uncle, when they were so clearly in love. She assured Kathleen that there was nothing either "priestly" or "uncle-ey" about the relationship.

So, Kathleen knew who her mother was. She was disappointed to learn that Ginny died a decade earlier. But now she knew that Ginny wanted to keep her, at least for a time. As Liz and Barb told her more about the Roethles, Kathleen had to dismantle and reconstruct the childish fairytale that she built. The Roethles weren't wealthy politicians, but strict, religious farmers.

I recalled what I knew of my Roethle ancestors. The Roethle family emigrated from the Bavarian region prior to 1840, and the Roethles were already well established for a good thirty years prior to the arrival of the Bohemian Biers on the scene. By contrast, the Roethles *were* wealthy, successful farmers. Their German community lived in Neosho, Wisconsin, a small village northwest of Milwaukee. Like the Biers, the Roethles were big into being Catholic and counted a smattering of nuns in their bunch. No priests, though.

Kathleen added that the modern Roethles were helpful, kind people to whom she felt an immediate kinship. She assumed that, surely, someone in that Roethle clan would know who her father was. Liz told Kathleen that two of her Aunt Ginny's seven siblings were still alive. One was Liz's own father, who was estranged from the family. Out of loyalty to Liz, Kathleen never tried to contact him. The other was the baby of the family, Jerome. Ginny's baby brother, Jerome, was 87 and living in a memory care unit in Wisconsin, with a son acting as his unofficial gatekeeper.

Surely between Jerome and his son, she'd get the answer. Kathleen soon discovered that Jerome was unable to communicate on his own. He suffered from dementia and required round-the-clock care. So, Kathleen tried his son, who she found on Facebook. His reply was brief. He just didn't want to talk about it, and that was that.

It was an unexpected response. Up until then, everyone she corresponded with was open and willing to help. Not deterred, Kathleen contacted Jerome's daughter-in-law, the terse son's wife. She suggested that her husband might be able to fill in gaps, but she couldn't force him to share what he knew. He would have to come around to it on his own time.

In the meantime, Kathleen and Liz started looking for clues in the 1,000+ other relatives that 23andme identified. One of these relatives had the last name Parr. Liz recalled that the Parrs were related to the Biers, and Liz remembered that one of the Biers became a Monsignor, Father Ed Bier. They drew some conclusions, contacted one of his relatives that made her work public— me—and the rest was history.

The hour and a half ballet class flew by, as I sat there in the cocoon of my car, chatting with Kathleen. I reluctantly wrapped up the conversation, "Well, I've gotta go. These kids are really cramping my style."

"Oh, don't say that; they're amazing. Just like their mom."

"We'll see about that...can't wait to meet you face to face." I replied and ended the call, jerking myself squarely into reality from the meandering trip down memory lane.

Casebook summary

FACTS

•Kathleen's father is almost certainly the priest who visited Ginny during her pregnancy

•Two of Ginny's brothers are still alive, but unwilling and/or unable to discuss their knowledge of her pregnancy

•The sham birth certificate names are a dead end
•Kathleen's father is somehow genetically related to a Dennis Parr

QUESTIONS

•What priests are related to Dennis Parr? Focus on Bier and Parr priests for now.
•How am I and the other Biers related Dennis Parr?
•When is Louise going to start analyzing Kathleen's DNA report?

Virginia "Ginny" Roethle, high school graduation.

The Leo and Helen (Bier) Roethle family. Ginny stands in the back
row, on the right. Jerome is seated on the footstool between his
parents. Liz's estranged father, Edward, is in the naval uniform.

Chapter Seven
Potential Priests

It was important to be as certain as possible that Kathleen's father was a priest, and now I was. Kathleen's father was the mysterious priest who visited Ginny during her stay with the Brummels; the priest was not Ginny's uncle. Further, Kathleen & Liz's interpretation of her DNA results was generally correct. Kathleen's father was someone in the larger Parr and/or Bier family trees. The next step was obvious: find a priest in that Bier and Parr tangle of branches.

In the average family, it would be easy to pinpoint such a person. In the Bier-Parr family tree, though, it was not that simple. In the Valentine Bier branch alone, there were six men that met the criteria in the timeframe. I went over what I knew of these six candidates' histories. This information was contained in my working family tree, as well as in documents and ephemera that my grandmother provided to my archives.

1. Father Charles Bier

It felt absolutely sacrilegious to place Father Charles on the candidate list, but completeness required his inclusion. If my great-uncle, Father Ed Bier, was held in high esteem by the family, my great-great uncle, Father Charles Bier, was downright revered. Charles Bier was a middle son of Valentine Bier—one of the original Valentine Ten. He was born in the old country, in Ketzelsdorf, and emigrated with the family at age two. He grew up to fulfill his devout parents' prayers and desires, when he was ordained in their new country. The expense of his seminary education was a burden shared by the entire family—and his success was equally shared and passed down through the generations, even to my own. The kids in my dad's generation were Father Charles' great nieces and nephews. All of them seemed to have at least one anecdote about this memorable character. Dad recalled learning chess from Father Charles, who also kept up numerous games by correspondence. He remembered terrifying rides as a passenger in Father Charles' Cadillac, which he learned to drive as he did a tractor: line up the hood ornament with the center line on the road and hope for the best.

Although I never met him, Father Charles was a real person to me, not just a static black and white image as so many other relatives of his generation were. I felt as though I knew him personally. The reason? The colorful anecdotes helped. But more importantly, my archives included over 30 years' worth of his meticulously handwritten diaries! In addition, he produced three volumes of memoirs based on these accounts. His written words were augmented by the hundreds of photographs he took. He was the original archivist for the Bier family— my progenitor in more ways than one. His writings gave such a rare, precious glimpse into the life of that family. They also provided a glimpse into him.

He was extraordinarily devout and proper. He loved chess, photography, and his Cadillac. I imagine that he also really loved the sound of his own voice. In some ways, Father Charles spoke directly to me across the centuries. In flights of fancy, I often thought that his inspiration drew me back into spirituality after years away from the church. If I was protective of Father Ed, I was *fiercely* protective of Father Charles.

Nevertheless, fair was fair. I tried to dispassionately consider him as a candidate. Father Charles Bier was 70 at the time of Kathleen's birth and already in failing health, after years of chronic tuberculosis. He lived in semi-retirement at St. Elizabeth's home for the elderly in Janesville, Wisconsin, taking care of the residents' spiritual needs while the sisters took care of his earthly ones. A cadre of local nuns managed the day-to-day affairs of the place. It wasn't a situation where a priest hired a private housekeeper, as parish priests did, so Ginny could not have kept house for him. Father Charles couldn't drive anymore and relied on his younger relatives to maintain his social calendar. He couldn't have been making secret jaunts back and forth, two hours each way, to Evanston, Illinois, to visit a pregnant Ginny. I considered him briefly, then I quickly eliminated Father Charles as the potential father. Whew.

2. Monsignor Edward (Ed) J. Bier

Father Ed was my great uncle who I considered previously. Given that I was examining the case with fresh eyes, I decided to consider him in the same light, despite my initial feelings of protection and indignation. He was in his early 30s at the time of Kathleen's conception, and stationed at two different parishes in the Madison, Wisconsin area; all of his parish assignments were in the diocese of Madison. His sister-in-law, nieces, and nephews did not recall him ever having a housekeeper named Ginny. This was notable, given that he was actually Ginny's cousin twice over (recall the dual Bier and Roethle marriages between their respective parents.) It seems like family would have known if his cousin was his housekeeper. I needed to confirm this assumption, however. For now, Father Ed's name remained on the list. Father Ed died in 1985 and is buried in the family plot in Mount Olivet Cemetery in Janesville, Wisconsin.

3. Father Robert (Bob) Bier

Father Bob is one of three priest-sons of Frank Bier, one of the Valentine Ten. Frank and Mary achieved a Catholic hat trick when three of their sons became priests. All of the sons in this family grew up in Janesville, Wisconsin, just a few miles from the Valentine Bier farm. All three brothers attended St. Francis Seminary, just south of Milwaukee. All three worked exclusively at community parishes in the Archdiocese of Milwaukee. Father Bob was in his late 40's at the time of Kathleen's birth, and assigned to a small parish in equally tiny Fredonia, Wisconsin. He died in 1995 and was buried in Johnsburg, Wisconsin.

4. Father Joseph (Joe) Bier

Father Joe was the second of the priest-sons of Frank and Mary Bier. He was in his early 40s at the time of Kathleen's birth and stationed at parishes in West Allis, a suburb of Milwaukee, and Brighton, a small town south of the city. He died in 1999 and was buried in Brighton, Wisconsin.

5. Father Francis (Fran) Bier

The third of the Frank and Mary Bier Catholic trifecta, Father Fran had the fewest notes in my files. He was in his mid 40s when Kathleen was born. I had no record of where he was stationed. He died in 1972 and was buried in Ashton, Wisconsin.

6. Father Robert (Bob) Gassert

Father Bob Gassert was another grandson of Valentine Bier. He was the son of Emily (Bier) Gassert and grew up in Milwaukee. He followed the Jesuit path, pursuing the intense, doctoral-level education required of that order of priesthood. He achieved academic success at Marquette University in Milwaukee, eventually becoming the Dean of the College of Liberal Arts. There were boxes and boxes of his papers housed in Marquette's archives. I never visited the archives, instead writing to obtain copies of some of documents that pertained to the family history. For example, he gave an address at the Golden Jubilee of his first cousin, Father Joseph Bier. My archives also contained a number of snapshots of him, as well as a stack of mass cards for various celebrations, and several copies of laudatory eulogies. He was in his early 30s at the time in question. I did not know where he was living at the time. He died in 1993 and is buried in Calvary Cemetery in Milwaukee.

So, in all, Valentine Bier had one son and five grandsons who became priests. These five men were all first cousins, or brothers, to each other. They were all first cousins or brothers to my own grandfather, Vince Bier. His wife, my Grandma Bier, had quite an impressive collection of information on Father Ed; he was her brother-in-law, after all. She had a ton on Father Charles, including all of those diaries which I was lucky enough to inherit. She left me a modest collection on Father Bob Gassert. The things which I inherited from her contained precious little information on the three priest brothers: Fathers Bob, Joe, and Fran. There were a couple funeral cards and one stray photo of Father Joseph Bier. She didn't even save obituary clippings for any of the three—and she saved obituaries on everyone. I have an entire file folder devoted to mysterious obituaries labeled, "who is this person???" But none for any of the three brother priests. Her notes contained little more than their names and nicknames. The absence was remarkable in contrast to the veritable sea of Catholic memorabilia that she saved for other relatives. The three were my Grandpa Bier's cousins, their childhood home was only a few miles from his. Why the echoing silence in the record? Also, why were none of the three sons buried at the traditional family plot at Mount Olivet in Janesville, along with their mother and father and countless other relatives?

After I reviewed my files on each of the potential priests, I revisited Father Charles' memoirs, which he self-effacingly titled "Memoirs of an Old Recluse." As I leafed through this 100+ page manuscript, volume one of three, I came across a provocative entry:

On Tuesday, July 4 [1899], we attended a Civic Celebration for Independence Day at Janesville. . ... On the next Sunday another set of visitors came to enjoy an outing at our house. Among them were . . .
Mr. Frank Bier (a widower) and his daughter Mary who later married Charles Parr and raised a family of 17 children, among them Father Raymond Parr and Sister M. Carol, O.P. [emphasis added] (Rev. Charles Bier, Memoirs of an Old Recluse).

Father Raymond Parr? So, there *was* at least one priest squarely in the Parr family tree. Talk about provocative. The list grew by one more.

* * *

This is as good a time as any to admit something: I knew a lot about these Bier priests. I suspect that most amateur genealogists have favorite family lines—branches of the tree that hold a greater allure than do others. This imbalance exists for me between my paternal grandfather's families. I'm equally Bier and Roethle, after all. Yet I never really connected with the Roethle history to the same degree as I did the Bier. First, I inherited so much more information on the Biers. More photos, more documents. Look at how easily I assembled dossiers on the potential priest fathers.

My own Grandma Bier left me so much Bier ephemera. I grew up in Janesville, surrounded by sites of Bier legend every day. And the diaries—oh, the diaries that Grandma Bier saved. I can physically touch words written by Biers 125 years ago. A lack of opportunities for similar connection with the Roethles explains most of the imbalance in my genealogical affections. Ultimately, though, I think a lot's in a name—my name is Bier, and it's a cool name.

That's not to say I don't feel *any* connection to the Roethles. I clearly know quite a bit about my Roethle ancestors. About eight years ago, I stopped for lunch with my then-toddler daughter at a restaurant in Milwaukee called the Honeypie Cafe. I was working on Roethle family history at the time, and my daughter helped me to insert photos into a scrapbook the night before. Luckily, she paid attention. During lunch, she set down her sandwich and pointed a chubby finger at a large, black and white photograph on the wall behind me.

She asked, "Hey, Mama, aren't those our family?" Sure enough, she was pointing out a two-by-three-foot photo of the Roethles.

As part of the cafe's old-timey decor, the Roethle family sat squarely in my daughter's sightline. The photograph was remarkably similar to a smaller one in my records; same day, different pose. It was astonishing, and I was pleased to know that my four-year old paid such close attention. After all, someone will eventually need to take over the archives. I mentioned the funny coincidence to our waitress, and eventually, word got back to the owner. Months later, he gave me the photo, which he bought at a flea market.

So, did I know a anything about the Roethle ancestors? Absolutely. I bet that I knew more than, at most, seven other people. But the Roethles were static images in a photograph on the wall of Honeypie Cafe. Now the Biers? I felt like I could start up a conversation with Valentine or any of the Valentine Ten, if they walked through the door.

The families were different in many ways, aside from the degree that I related to them. The Roethles were Bavarian Germans, the Biers Bohemian Germans. To our modern minds, this sounds like an insignificant difference. At the time, though, the communities were very insular. In Wisconsin, the Biers and Roethles lived more than 60 miles apart—more than a day's journey by horse and cart. The Roethles were a settled, prosperous clan. The Biers lived hand to mouth, especially in the early days.

The feat of the double Bier-Roethle marriages was accomplished due to the intercession of Father Charles Bier, the original Bier priest. At some point, he was assigned to a parish in the village of Rubicon, near the home of the Roethle family. Father Charles decided that a Roethle girl would make an excellent bride for his as-yet unmarried youngest brother, Edward. Rosalia Roethle and Edward Bier married, eventually giving rise to The Four Bier Boys. It didn't take long for Rosalia's younger brother, Leo, to follow suit and marry a Bier of his own, one of Edward's nieces, Helen Bier.

So, Father Charles was the culprit in the unlikely double Bier-Roethle marriages. Which of the other priests on the list was also a father?

Casebook summary
FACTS

•In addition to the priests in the Valentine Bier family, there is at least one priest in the Parr family as well-Father Raymond Parr

QUESTIONS

•What's the story on Father Raymond Parr?
•Where were all of the potential priests at the time of Kathleen's birth?
•How are the Biers and Parrs related?

Potential Fathers

Charles Bier

Edward Bier

Francis Bier

Joseph Bier

Robert Bier

Robert Gassert

Raymond Parr

Father Charles Bier, taken around the time of Kathleen's birth

Father Charles Bier at his first mass. The young girl is his niece, Helen Bier, who would eventually marry Leo Roethle and become Ginny Roethle's mother.

Father Charles Bier & his nephew, Father Robert Gassert

Monsignor Edward J. Bier around the time of his ordination

Father Robert Gassert, around the time of his ordination

Father Joseph Bier, around the time of his retirement

Photo of the John and Katherine Roethle family from my archives...

. . . and the one from the Honeypie Cafe.

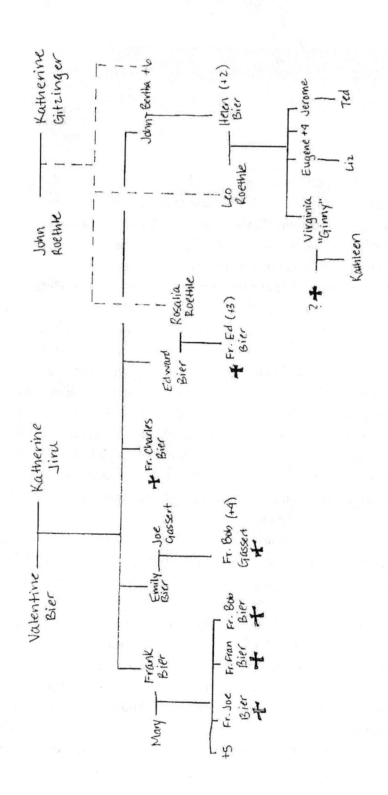

Chapter Eight
The Parr Question

Of the open questions in my casebook, I was uniquely suited to answer one in particular, "How are Kathleen and the rest of the Biers related to the Parrs?" Dennis Parr's presence in Kathleen's 23andme report was the best link to her biological father. I understood genetics and the Bier family tree. I did not understand the Parr family tree. In searching through my files, I found a ten-year-old note on my to-do list: "figure out the Parr - Bier connection." Huh. Too bad I never got around to that. I needed to query a fellow researcher who had knowledge of the Parr tree. Knowing none, that meant turning to Ancestry.com.

Ancestry.com has been around for awhile, well before it got into the commercial DNA game. It is a website for doing genealogy research, charting one's growing tree, and sharing results with other researchers. There are aspects of working on Ancestry that I really enjoy. Ancestry catalogues scores of primary sources, many of which include images of the original documents. In the past, genealogists spent a lot of time in small historical libraries, poring through handwritten documents to access documents like these. Ancestry makes a lot of these references available and easily searchable from one's computer. Don't get me wrong—I still love a morning spent buried in the stacks of a small local library, and this type of research remains absolutely necessary. But slowly, Ancestry is digitizing these libraries' troves.

Another nice feature of Ancestry are the green-leaf hints. Once you have even basic elements of your tree input into the site, it starts feeding you hints upon hints upon hints based upon those names and dates. The hints appear as enticing green leaves next to your relatives' names, just begging to be clicked and chased down. And it's so easy to go down the rabbit hole of these green leaf hints. They might lead to other peoples' trees, census records, social security death records, any number of records that may or may not have something to do with the relative flagged with a green leaf. On more than one occasion, my husband tried to tear my attention away from the seduction of an Ancestry green leaf, commenting, "You are more interested in dead people than in us." It's the green leaves. They are irresistible!

The problem with the seductive green leaves, though, is that Ancestry makes it almost too easy to add their suggestions to your research. There is no one reminding you to "double-check your info," before merging it into your rapidly-growing tree. This danger is especially true when it comes to incorporating data from other members' trees. While it is possible to build a tree on Ancestry privately, users are encouraged to share their work publicly. Then, any possible overlap between different people's trees sparks green leaf hints. A few clicks, and some anonymous person's data is grafted onto the other's tree. What often ends up happening is that multiple people share the same data and family trees, repeatedly copying and pasting from the original researcher who created the tree in the first place. Did that original person use good, verified data? Who knows. And Ancestry doesn't clear its throat loudly to alert you to the fact that you might be making a mistaken graft. Instead, it lulls you into a click-happy trance with all of those green leaves.

I tread lightly when it comes to trusting other members' trees. And I never, never graft them onto my own. Call me snobbish, but I don't want to accidentally taint all of my carefully sourced work. I also keep my own tree private; it is invisible to other users of Ancestry. I learned the hard way that not everyone may agree with the version of the truth as represented in my tree.

In addition to putting in names and dates, I populate my tree with all sorts of decorative fruits and flowers—pictures, maps, documents, and stories. While I don't present the stories as biographical facts, I do include them as attachments. About ten years ago, I uploaded my tree and shared it on Ancestry, and I mistakenly included everything—facts and anecdotes alike. Unfortunately, one of the anecdotes was about a distant relative who, according to my great-aunts, killed herself "because her husband brought home a venereal disease." This little tidbit was nestled away in my public Ancestry tree. Eventually, a descendent of that woman discovered it and wrote me a scathing message about posting such gossipy information publicly. Mortified, I deleted my public tree altogether and stayed completely away from Ancestry for years out of shame and trepidation. I still had genealogy management software on my own computer on which I continued to grow my tree; I just never synced it up to Ancestry online.

Well, it was time to return. I renewed my Ancestry subscription and dove back into the familiar, overwhelming Ancestry.com website. My ultimate goal was to determine if the connection between Kathleen and Dennis Parr was a clue to her biological father's whereabouts in the Bier-Parr tree, which I had yet to build. I searched for users' Parr family trees. I eventually found several and started wading through them.

I quickly found the Bier-Parr connection. In all of the online Parr trees, "Frank Bier" was the founding Wisconsin ancestor. *My* Frank Bier. Frank Bier of the Valentine Ten. He of the amazing cheekbones. He with the three priest sons. Frank Bier appeared as the father of "Mary Bier" (mother unknown). Mary Bier eventually married a Charles Parr and established the Parr dynasty of southern Wisconsin.

This was news to me. As far as my records indicated, Frank Bier had neither a daughter named Mary nor a Parr relationship. According to everything I knew, he was married only once, to Mary Klein, and never had a daughter named Mary. The Parr trees included this marriage to Mary Klein along with all of its associated children, but as a second marriage.

Was it possible that Frank Bier was actually married twice, a fact heretofore overlooked in my Bier research? Or did he father a daughter named Mary out of wedlock?

A quick review of the facts as presented on these Parr trees answered my questions: no way. My Frank Bier, of the Valentine Ten, was only 11 years old at the time that Mary Bier, matriarch of the Parrs, was born. She simply couldn't have been his daughter. *It wasn't the same Frank Bier—there must have been two of them!* The founder of the Parr family was a different Frank Bier, and all of these Parr family trees were mixing him up with Frank of the Valentine Ten!

Here's how it might have happened. Somewhere along the line, a researcher noticed that Mary Bier's father was named Frank, that Valentine Bier had a son named Frank, and created a tree showing both of these Frank Biers as the same person. And then Ancestry encouraged people to copy and paste the mistake, and no one ever bothered to check the math. Repeated enough times, the idea that the Parrs were descended from Valentine Bier via his son, Frank, became an accepted truth. Later, I learned that this conflation and assumption appeared on handwritten charts shared between Parr family members for years, well before the advent of Ancestry.com. I wanted to shout this discovery from the rooftops. There are two Frank Biers! You've got the wrong guy! But alas, Ancestry does not have a town crier function.

So, who was this other Frank Bier, whose daughter co-founded the Wisconsin Parr dynasty? I started referring to him as Mystery Frank while I attempted to sort it out. I discovered a census record indicating that Mystery Frank lived in Rock County in 1860, prior to the arrival of the Valentine Biers in 1882. I confirmed this on an 1860 plat map. In 1860, Mystery Frank Bier owned a 40-acre parcel, 10 miles from the eventual Valentine Bier homestead. Mystery Frank and Valentine must have been related somehow, but not in a son-father relationship. Now the question was, where did Mystery Frank graft onto my own Valentine Bier family tree?

Before I went any further, I had to share my discovery, town crier or not.

From: Me
To: Liz

Liz,
I was just trying to figure out how Frank Bier (Valentine's son) had any relation to the Parrs in question. I found some trees on Ancestry.com

that show that Frank had a daughter named Mary who married a Parr, and that's the connection. Problem: The Mary Bier that started the Parrs in Janesville was born when <u>our</u> Frank Bier, from the Valentine family, was only 11. . . Someone made this "mystery" Frank Bier the Frank Bier from the Valentine Bier family, but they've made an error, and everyone just copies each other's work on Ancestry and can perpetuate errors. Either way, we need to unpack Kathleen's DNA relation to the Parrs, because if she has it and you don't, it's the key, I think. However, I don't think the connection is via the Frank Bier of Valentine Bier. See what I'm saying? I wish I were sitting here with you to talk through this.

AB

From: Liz
To: Me

Hi, Angela!
I see what you're saying. Kathleen has spoken to Dennis Parr —he and his wife own a winery up in the state of Washington.... they've talked on the phone about the family tree, although that doesn't mean they are correct. The only data I have is the same — Frank [Bier] married somebody and had a daughter Mary who married Charles Parr [. . .] But if this isn't the correct Frank Bier, son of Valentine Bier ....Hmmmm.... Interesting that this could be a link to unlock something. . ..

Liz

I had to construct a Parr tree that went all the way back to the common ancestor between the Mystery Frank Bier and Valentine Bier. In addition, it needed to go far enough forward to accurately outline the modern-day Parrs, including Dennis Parr, Kathleen's DNA relative, and Father Raymond Parr, one of the potential priest fathers. I must know someone in the Parr family. My trusty genealogy contacts database gave me the answer, Dick Bier.

Explaining who Dick Bier is will be another trip down the lane of "multiple marriages between families." The first connection is with Mystery Frank Bier; his daughter, Mary, married Charles Parr and had a boatload of kids. Well, in addition, Louis Bier, of the Valentine Ten, married Charles Parr's sister, Frances, and had only a small dinghy-load of children. Louis was the third eldest child of the Valentine Ten, and he also farmed around Janesville and still has numerous relatives scattered in the area. One of them was his grandson, Dick Bier. Dick was a frequent, thoughtful commenter on my blog. I quickly located Dick's information and sent off a note.

From: Me
To: Richard Bier

Hi Dick—
I recently had some interesting correspondence with a woman who found me through the blog. Long story short, she was adopted and has identified her birth mother (who is related to me by virtue of being a Roethle), and her father is somehow related to Dennis Parr, as evidenced by DNA. There was a lot of back and forth involving the fact that she thought that the Frank Bier that was Dennis' relative was the Frank Bier of the Valentine 10. However, he is the mysterious "Uncle Frank Bier." I was going through old correspondence and found that in 2008 (gasp, 10 years ago?) you were wondering about the same question. I'm curious—did you ever find an answer? Who is this Uncle Frank?

I think he's more than a titular uncle. His census records show him progressively identifying his country of origin as Germany, then Bohemia, then the Czech Republic. Same region as the Valentine Biers and Ketzelsdorf. However, I wonder if he's something other than an actual brother of Valentine? It just seems strange that he wouldn't have helped out his own brother at all in those first few years, and his name doesn't seem to surface until later, although this is based on

Father Charles' Memoirs; there is no daily diary until 1899. Gaaaah, I love genealogy.

This correspondence with the adopted daughter has been an interesting exercise in the real-world consequences of poorly done genealogy, DNA work, etc., etc. Half of the family trees on Ancestry have "Uncle" Frank and Frank of the Valentine 10 coalesced into one person, and this Frank having fathered a single daughter with an unknown woman at the age of 11.!!!!!

From: Richard Bier
To: Me

Angela,
Thank you for your very interesting message. I, too, have heard, via email, from the woman who is searching for her father. I don't think I told her anything she doesn't already know. If she is Helen Bier Roethle's grandchild, then she and I share great-grandparents, namely, Valentine and Catherine. Since her DNA had indicated a connection to a Parr, I pointed out the Bier-Parr alliance in the Louis Bier branch in that my grandfather married Frances Parr and her brother, Charles, married Mary Bier. Your hypothesis that the "non-ten" Frank Bier might have been a brother to Valentine and Anton seems plausible. I can clearly remember my father referring to Uncle Ed and Aunts Frances, Amalia, and Em. He also mentioned Uncle Anton who, of course, was his great uncle. I never heard of any Uncle Frank be it of the ten or a possible brother to Valentine. Getting a firm answer to the "Parr-Bier" question remains unsolved, at least for me. I expect the answer lies in the Parr family.

Dick

Dick's note mentions the tricky fact that I tried to avoid: Kathleen already has a connection to the Bier family by virtue of her maternal great-grandparents. With any potential Bier or Parr father, it would be difficult to tease out how much Bier-ness came from her mother's relationship and how much from her father's. All the more reason to keep my sister, Louise, well in the loop. It was also tricky because Kathleen's parents were themselves somehow related. All of the potential priests on the list were some degree of a cousin to Ginny. Gulp.

While Dick focused on acquiring accurate modern-day data, I looked to the past. I knew where I needed to focus my search. Alverno College in Milwaukee & the Zamrsk Archives in the Czech Republic.

Casebook summary

FACTS

•There are no accurate records of how the Bier and Parr families are related.

QUESTIONS

•So, how are the Biers and Parrs related? Where does Mystery Frank Bier fit in?
•What about Father Raymond Parr? Dennis Parr?

Potential Fathers

Edward Bier	Francis Bier
Robert Gassert	~~Charles Bier~~
Robert Bier	Raymond Parr
Joseph Bier	

The boys of the Valentine Ten. Seated: Father Charles Bier. Standing, left to right: Edward Bier (my great-grandfather, dad of Father Ed), Louis Bier (also married a Parr), John Bier (daughter, Helen, became Helen Roethle, mother of Ginny), and Frank (amazing cheekbones. Father of the three priest brothers).

I have no photos of "Mystery Frank" Bier.

1

Chapter Nine
Alverno to Zamrsk

I didn't have to work too hard to attach Dennis Parr to the Parr family tree. Come to find out, Kathleen already reached out to him through 23andme. Dennis' wife responded and provided Kathleen with what information she had on the Parr family tree. Unfortunately, this information carried the same erroneous Bier-Parr connection that I found online. It did, however, have much more accurate information on the modern members of the Parr family. The mystery of how Dennis Parr was related to Father Raymond Parr was solved.

Charles and Mary (Bier) Parr, daughter of Mystery Frank Bier, had 18 children, an amazing 16 of whom survived to adulthood. One of these children was Father Raymond Parr. Another was Harold Parr, father of Dennis from 23andme. Once I alerted Kathleen to the presence of a priest in the Parr lineage, she immediately contacted Nancy Parr for information. Nancy sent along a few other clues.

From: Kathleen LeFranc
Fwd: from Nancy Parr
To: Me

Father Raymond A. Parr was Dennis's fraternal uncle: [link to an obituary] Then there's a book: Father Raymond A. Parr: priest of the Archdiocese of Milwaukee, WI, from 1939-2002.

Don't know if that helps. Dennis said he also had a parish in Racine, WI.

Best, Nancy

Yes, Nancy, this helped immensely. First, it connected Dennis and Raymond Parr as nephew and uncle. So, if Father Raymond was Kathleen's father, then Dennis Parr would be her first cousin. I had to go back and check whether that squared with the 23andme results. In the meantime, I needed to look into Father Raymond Parr's biography. The obituary said that he was a chaplain at Alverno, a small college in Milwaukee. The only copy of the biography that she mentioned was in Alverno's library. It was written by a religious order, the School Sisters of St. Francis. Had Father Raymond served as a teacher for this order? Could Ginny have been his student during her brief sojourn into religious life? The only sure way to find out was a field trip to Alverno College.

As I drove to Alverno, I anticipated sketching a picture of Father Raymond Parr. Like all of the others on the "potential fathers" list, he was dead. Instead of personal interviews, I had to get a sense of the man from archival materials, along with recollections from his living relatives. In reality, I would have to do this for all of the priests on the potential fathers list. Except, of course, for Father Charles, who I already eliminated.

I drove by Alverno in the past, usually when taking the back roads from my south-side suburban home to a Brewer's game. I thought that it was a women's college for nontraditional students, i.e., mid-career women. A quick review of Alverno's website revealed that the college was, in fact, an all-women's Catholic college, and that it was originally chartered by the School Sisters of St. Francis. This explained why Father Raymond's biography was authored by that order. He most likely did not work with that order's student nuns.

I pulled into the college's parking lot and passed a number of students, young and older, heading toward cars. I also saw several residence halls. In reality, Alverno was a mix of residential and commuter, traditional and non-traditional. I stopped two young women to ask for directions to the library, and they sent me through a main entrance which spilled out onto a sidewalk. Across the street marched a row of neat Milwaukee bungalows. I walked up the wide steps, pausing in the academically cool hallway to let my eyes adjust to the dimness. I glanced ahead of me at an empty chapel. I walked down a carpeted hallway and entered the library, which was relatively high-ceilinged and airy in comparison to the preceding space. I had the call number of Father Parr's biography, and handed it over to the student working the desk. She located the slim volume and said that, "No, you don't need to sign in. You can sit anywhere." So, I did.

I quickly realized that this biography of Father Raymond Parr was more of an homage than a scholarly work. I had to take everything I read with a grain of salt. That being said, there were still plenty of cold, hard facts. Raymond Parr was born in 1915, the fourth of the 18 children born to Charles and Mary Parr. Mary was originally Mary Bier, the daughter of "Mystery" Frank Bier and a never-named mother. By all accounts, the Parrs were a remarkably hard-working family that lived on a farm east of Janesville, Wisconsin. Raymond began his schooling in a one-room district school at age four, to which he was admitted early because the school needed one more student in order to stay open. He transferred to St. Mary's parish school in third grade, and graduated at age 11, having skipped a grade. There, he and his siblings would have frequently crossed paths with their relatives in the Valentine Bier family (1).

Life in the Charles and Mary Parr household read like historical fiction. The picture painted was of a family that was poor, practical, and hard-working:

"Raymond's father once took him to see the burning crosses of the Ku Klux Klan on the prairies around Janesville. That frightening experience was so pivotal that he recalled it later in life, saying that if left a deep impression on him. That same father was named "Father of the Year" in 1949 by a women's club in Janesville. Comments in the article on the event give some insight into what life was like in that large family."

... the Parrs speak endlessly on the subject of family cooperation; how the first eight children were boys, and how these rotated week by week sharing the dishwashing chores, and the countless household tasks, and about the 200-foot washline filled twice each washday, two washdays a week. Cooking and baking quantities were of restaurant proportions. (1.)

How on earth had this shoestring-surviving family managed to save enough money to pay for Raymond's seminary education? He attended St. Francis Seminary in Milwaukee, like so many of the Bier family priests. Similarly, upon ordination, he celebrated his first mass at the home parish of St. Mary's in Janesville. For his first assignment, from 1939-1953, he was stationed at a Bohemian parish where many of the parishioners still spoke Czech. Next, he was very briefly employed at a parish in Milwaukee, before assuming a role at Alverno College in 1953 as chaplain and professor. Alverno maintained a strong connection with the nearby School Sisters of St. Francis' convent. However, Father Raymond never had an official appointment at the mother house itself.

In terms of opportunities for Ginny to have been his housekeeper, the only period was while he was at the Bohemian parish, St. John Nepomuk, on the south side of Milwaukee. As soon as he began working at Alverno, the School Sisters of St. Francis would have attended to his meals, laundry, etc. These sisters came to the campus in the morning and left in the evening, residing off-site at their convent, while he stayed on campus. When I envisioned a situation in which Ginny was able to have an affair with a priest, it required their actually living under the same roof. I further speculated that it had to be an isolated residence with few, if any, other occupants. In the life of Father Raymond Parr, his time at St. John Nepomuk was the only realistic opportunity.

Father Raymond Parr taught at Alverno for the remainder of his career. By all accounts, he was universally admired, both for his open-door friendliness, astonishing wisdom, and insight. While his biography was certainly written with a slant toward admiration, it nonetheless provided numerous specific examples to support its thesis. On the occasion of his Golden Jubilee, or 50 years of priesthood, a friend attempted to capture him in a poem:

> He is light to
> illumine our shadows, for
> We who tarry in
> The dimness are drawn
> To luminescence by the
> Power of his word.
> We who fall—and
> Sometimes we fall—stretch toward
> His tall thoughts to
> Heal, renew, inspire.
> Led
> By his vision and
> Aware that "no one
> Can stay in any
> Golden moment" we pray
> The spirit light him
> To the eternal word.
> S. Kevin Robertson
> 1989 (1)

From 1979 until his death in 1999, Father Raymond "retired" from Alverno and became a professor emeritus. Throughout his retirement, he continued to coordinate campus ministries, teach adult classes, and write a book. He also pursued furniture building, home remodeling, art collection, and cookery. He was described as modern, intelligent, beloved, and an institution. The more I learned, the more it seemed that Father Raymond was the antithesis of a man harboring a dark secret. His active, outwardly-reaching life seemed singularly incompatible with subterfuge of any sort.

I spent the better part of an afternoon in the Alverno library, the shadows growing long through the large windows as students came and went around me. In the end, nothing in Father Raymond's biographical information or papers suggested a time when he might have carried on an illicit affair with Ginny Roethle, save for those pesky few years at St. John Nepomuk, which needed a bit more review. His involvement with students was full of glowing reports, not even a whiff of impropriety. He never directly supervised any nuns-in-training, despite the School Sisters of St. Francis being the printers of his biography. I packed up my things, notes and copies in hand. I returned the slim volumes at the desk. On the way out, I stopped in the Alverno chapel. It was empty, save for the familiar flickering warmth of a few candles at side altars. On the left of the main altar was a small altar dedicated to the Virgin Mother. I stopped, knelt down, and brought to mind mothers: my own, my friend whose son was struggling, Ginny Roethle and her daughter, Kathleen McHugh.

In regards to Father Raymond Parr, the final question that needed answering was the genealogical relationship between the Parrs and the Biers. I had Raymond Parr's relationship to Dennis Parr and Mary Bier straightened out. Now I just had to ascertain how Mary and her father, Mystery Frank Bier, connected to the Valentine Bier family tree. Then, my geneticist sister and I could compare the way the Kathleen LeFranc and Dennis Parr were actually related with how they should be related if Father Raymond Parr were her father.

* * *

During the Bier Trip to the Homeland the previous summer, our bus briefly stopped in the Czech hamlet of Zamrsk. Our tour guide arranged the stop to show me the building where parish records from the outlying Bohemian village churches were archived. She warned me that I wouldn't be able to enter—the hours were limited and appointments were required. However, she assured me, all of the records were digitized and available online. She shared a copy of Valentine Bier's baptismal record that she made from the digitized archives, reassuring me that they were quite easy to navigate. Resigned, I gazed at the outside of the archives building, a renovated prison. As the group stretched our collective legs, a few of us happened on a family picnic and were offered beers—the drinkable kind. We continued on our way to Ketzelsdorf; I added Zamrsk Digital Archives to my genealogy to-do list for a later day.

When we returned home, I fully intended to spend time with those digital records. However, I was daunted. The files were numerous. They were catalogued in Czech. They were handwritten in German. They were simply overwhelming. Without a specific question, there was no hook to lure me into tackling these dense archives. With the Kathleen mystery, however, I had a specific task: Find Valentine Bier. Find Mystery Frank Bier. Find their common ancestor. Solve the mystery of the Bier-Parr relationship.

I dove into the digital fray of the Archives at Zamrsk.

First, I downloaded all of the zip files for the village of Ketzelsdorf. There were about 20 unique file sets, each containing a different church record book. These record books were handwritten in German, hundreds of years ago. I identified a promising register, baptisms, and opened it. I stared in transfixed horror at the pages that might as well have been hieroglyphics. I couldn't turn to Google translate for help, because I couldn't even decipher the letters of the German words! They were a series of inky tracings, meaningless loops and whorls!

Desperate, I Googled things like "how can I translate these old German registers?" or "deciphering old German text for the non-German speaker." Miraculously, I found a self-published book amusingly titled, *If I Can, You Can Decipher Germanic Records.* It might as well have been the Rosetta Stone itself!

If Edna M. Bentz hadn't written this book, I'm not sure that I would have ever been able to make any sense of the Zamrsk archives. Edna's miraculous volume gave translations for words frequently used in genealogy, such as "date," "birth," "death," and "legitimate." I made a list of the words that I needed to be on the lookout for, such as *Taufe* for baptism and *Mutter* for mother. Perhaps most importantly, the book provided examples of every way that a letter might be written in the German script common to the 18th and 19th centuries. There was an entire page of variations devoted to each letter—a separate page for capital and lower-case. The variation was overwhelming! I felt how today's school children must feel when confronted with cursive writing. I wanted to reach out to Edna and thank her personally. Unfortunately, she died several years before I discovered her book.

My next big breakthrough was discovering that one of the scanned books was a master index of births. It referenced all the other volumes, listing only the barest of facts and page numbers. The actual registers of births, deaths and baptisms were much wordier and therefore more confusing. I had no chance of deciphering these sentences, even with my handy translation book. The master index, however, was far less wordy and far more uniform: name, date, parents' names and birthdates, house number. And there were only a few words, generally names or numbers, in each uniform, predictable column. This was it! I had only to turn to the "B" section and find Frank and Valentine Bier!

Except that there was at least one index page of Biers *per year*. I had a vague notion that Ketzelsdorf had a lot of Biers, but this was absolutely insane. At least 30 Bier babies were born per year in the tiny village. Further, the same given names were repeated over and over— about six common names each for boys and girls. There were half a dozen Franz [Frank] Biers born per year in Ketzelsdorf. I clearly wouldn't be able to just scan for the names I wanted and go from there; there was simply too much repetition. How to find Mystery Frank and Valentine needles in the haystack of Biers?

Luckily, the births index contained one more important data point for each entry, a house number. House numbering became common in Europe during the mid-18th century, and the same numbering system survives in many places to this day—including Ketzelsdorf. Therefore, I logicked, assuming that families didn't tend to move around very much, I could identify family units by combining patterns of three variables: mother's name, father's name, and house number.

It was time. Time for a sortable document. Time for a spreadsheet. Over the next month, whenever I had a spare minute or two, I'd pull up the "B" section of the baptismal register and enter data for the Bier babies. I knew that Valentine was born in 1842 and Mystery Frank in

1844, so I catalogued 1800 to 1850, hoping to capture them, their parents, and their grandparents.

I couldn't concentrate on this task for very long at one sitting. It simultaneously required immense focus and was terribly boring. The data entry portion was boring, but the deciphering of script was incredibly difficult, even with Edna's useful book. I added several new versions of lettering to those that she provided as I progressed, as different handwriting appeared. The index contained page-years of "legible" script, followed abruptly by years of chicken scratch, corresponding to the arrival of a new parish priest. In the end, I filled a lot of fields with question marks, never quite settling on what certain scribbles meant. For example, it took me about a month to realize that what I thought was a "G" was actually a "Th." A whole world of "Theresias" was opened to me. I only hoped that I had enough useable data mixed with the question marks to identify the family trends that I needed.

In the end, I entered data on 380 Biers born in Ketzelsdorf between 1800-1850. Then I had to make sense of it, and shake Mystery Frank Bier and Valentine Bier out of the pile of names. One stroke of luck was the name "Valentine." His parents were creative namers in a sea of uniformity. There was only one "Valentin" born in the entire time span that I catalogued, on February 14, 1842. They named him for the saint whose feast day he shared. When I found his entry, I was relieved. The register's information matched with what I had in my records, down to the house number in which he was born—number 78.

A second stroke of luck? I knew the name of Valentine's brother, Anton. I found an Anton with the same parents as Valentine, Johann and Victoria Bier. Strangely, Anton was born in number 136, not number 78 like Valentine. When Valentine was born, his family lived with his maternal grandparents at number 78. After that, they moved in with their paternal grandparents at number 136, where Anton was born. Number 136 was actually the Bier family home, the place where all of the answers resided. If I didn't know that Valentine and Anton were brothers, I would have entirely ignored number 136.

Once I identified the correct Bier household, it was relatively simple to identify all the babies and parents of number 136, back to Valentine's grandparents. Long story short? Valentine Bier and Mystery Frank Bier were first cousins. They shared a common grandfather, the delightfully named Adalbert Bier. Recall that Mystery Frank Bier's daughter was the matriarch of the Parr dynasty. Although there was nowhere to do so, I could finally announce that the Biers and the Parrs were rather distantly related indeed, back to number 136 in Ketzelsdorf and Adalbert Bier in the late 1700s. Whew.

This was vital in interpreting the 23andme results. If Father Raymond Parr was Kathleen's father, she and Dennis should be first cousins. If he was not her father, their sole connection was through the great-great-great grandfather Adalbert Bier, and Kathleen and Dennis Parr should be fourth cousins. According to 23andme, Kathleen and Dennis shared less than 2% of their DNA. First cousins share around 10%. Fourth cousin share around 2%. Boom. This seemingly eliminated Father Raymond Parr from the possibility of being Kathleen's father.

Despite this, I wasn't quite ready to publicly eliminate Father Raymond from the list. I suppose it was all those years of scientific and medical training. It's just so darn hard, if not impossible, to prove a negative. There were still the confusing factors of Kathleen likely having two sources of Bier blood—through her mom and her dad. How to account for this? The models used by 23andme certainly didn't. I needed my geneticist sister, Louise.

From: Kathleen LeFranc
To: Me

Angie,
I'm thrilled that Louise is involved in trying to solve this genetic mystery!
Kathleen

PS: We do have a couple things in common. Your sister at Columbia! Two of my children went to Brown University. My daughter attended for her undergrad and my son for his Masters. They are both writers. My son started out as a playwright in New York. He won the *New York Times* "Best New Playwright of the Year" award (2010). Both he and my daughter are now in Los Angeles and are both TV writers. It's quite the gift you share!

Of course, I updated Louise on all these developments, both genealogical, genetic, and IMDB-related. Like me, she was reluctant to declare a "genetic solution" to the problem until we had time to sit down with the data. In the meantime, I privately crossed Father Raymond Parr off my list. I couldn't imagine a way that Louise's genetics programs could account for Kathleen and Dennis Parr not being related enough. If anything, Kathleen's double dollop of Bier blood should make them more related than predicted, not less.

In eliminating Father Raymond, I was relieved. With all I learned about Father Raymond Parr, I grew to have a fair amount of scholarly and personal admiration for the guy. Like my Great Uncle Father Ed, I now felt protective of this man's reputation.

Casebook summary

FACTS

• I'm almost certain that Father Raymond Parr is not Kathleen's father
  o Kathleen and Dennis Parr should have shown up as first cousins on 23andme if Father Raymond Parr were her father—and they definitely do not.
• The Parrs were related through a common grandfather between Valentine and "Mystery Frank."

oAny Wisconsin Biers, therefore, would show a distant relationship to any Wisconsin Parr.

Potential Fathers

Edward Bier
Robert Gassert
Robert Bier
Joseph Bier
Francis Bier
~~Charles Bier~~
~~Raymond Parr~~

An example of a more legible page from one of the baptism registers from the Zamrsk Archives.

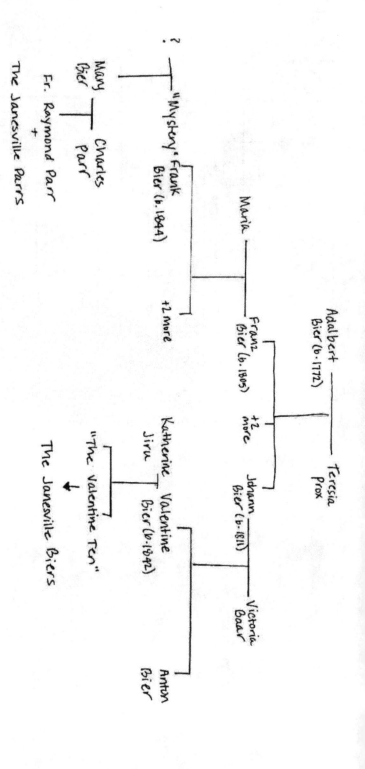

? — "Mystery" Frank Bier (b. 1844)

Mary Bier — Charles Parr

Fr. Raymond Parr
+
The Janesville Parrs

Maria — Franz Bier (b. 1805)

+2 more

Adalbert Bier (b. 1772) — Teresia Prox

+2 more

Johann Bier (b. 1811) — Victoria Baar

Katherine Jira — Valentine Bier (b. 1842)

Anton Bier

"The Valentine Ten"

The Janesville Biers

Father Raymond Parr at his ordination, complete with the traditional German youths. (courtesy of Father Raymond A. Parr : priest of the Archdiocese of Milwaukee, WI)

Father Raymond Parr. (courtesy of Father Raymond A. Parr: priest
of the Archdiocese of Milwaukee, WI)

Chapter Ten
DNA, Data, and Dead Ends

My visit to Alverno College prompted a visit to another site related to several of the potential fathers, St. Francis Seminary. On my list of potential priests, all but two (Father Edward Bier and Father Robert Gassert) studied there. I visited on several previous occasions and was happy to return to the imposing stone edifice and breathtaking views.

The seminary commands prime real estate in Milwaukee County, hugging the picturesque shores of Lake Michigan. It has been there since 1856, and the Archdiocese of Milwaukee's offices reside on the adjacent property. The seminary was established in 1845, prior to occupying its current location. The Archdiocese started the seminary to churn out "urgently needed" priests for all the German Catholic immigrants in the greater Milwaukee area (7). The School Sisters of St. Francis, the same order of sisters who founded Alverno College, donated the land for the seminary's eventual lakeside spot.

The first of the Bier priests to train at St. Francis Seminary was Father Charles Bier. He enrolled in 1898 and studied there until his ordination in 1905, returning to the Valentine Bier home farm in the summers. In those years, the seminary was high school, college, and divinity program all rolled into one. Father Charles wrote extensively of his time at the Seminary in his memoirs, recalling teachers and classmates by name. My first visit to the Seminary years ago was to drop off a copy of his memoirs for their archives; they were full of details and anecdotes that needed to be shared.

After Father Charles, Raymond Parr studied there, as did the three brother priests, Fathers Robert, Francis, and Joseph Bier. At the very least, a visit could confirm these men's ordination dates. I also planned to find out whether Father Paul McArdle ever enrolled at the Seminary. Father Paul orchestrated Ginny's placement during her pregnancy with

Kathleen, and Kathleen's subsequent adoption by the McHughs. I still had a hard time figuring out how the priest-father identified Father Paul's parish as the place to go to seek placement for Ginny. If he were a classmate of one of the potential fathers, that would be a significant clue.

Now that my oldest daughter was 12 years old, I felt comfortable leaving her and her sister home alone for several hours at a time. One lazy summer afternoon, I left them lolling around the cool basement and drove to St. Francis. I entered the main stone building and approached the receptionist who greeted me with a benign smile. I explained that I was doing family research, and I was interested in confirming the dates of enrollment of several priests. I thought it best to avoid sharing all the details of my search; I guessed that neither St. Francis Seminary nor the Archdiocese of Milwaukee would be anxious to help solve the mystery of which of their priests secretly fathered a child. I wrote down the names of the men in whom I was interested, handed them to the archivist, and went to wait in the reception area.

The waiting room was minimally furnished, save for an elevated table with an enormous, gilt-edged book on top. The volume was a photo album, documenting all the graduating classes of the Seminary through the years. Sure enough, I found Father Charles' familiar face with the class of 1905. I also found photos of the other four priests and snapped pictures on my phone. It was the first time I saw images of the two of the three Bier brother priests. I knew very little about them. It was good to finally have faces to put to their names. Notably, Father Paul McArdle was nowhere to be found.

The archivist returned in short order, bearing several index cards, one for each of the priests of interest. The cards recorded, in neat Palmer method handwriting, the dates of enrollment and graduation. There was no Paul McArdle anywhere in her records, at any level of education. Another dead end. Now I had a visual for each of the potential fathers. None of them looked like Kathleen, but then again, she was almost wholly Ginny in appearance. Visual clues would not be helpful in linking Kathleen to a father.

As I learned more about the potential fathers, I constructed timelines for each of them. In a spreadsheet, of course. I knew the complete chronology for Fathers Charles, Ed, and Raymond. I highlighted their whereabouts during the time when Kathleen was conceived. There were glaring absences in the chronologies of the three Bier brothers. Luckily, I knew where the answer lay: at the Archdiocese of Milwaukee. I consulted their website and found a request form for their archivist. Given some of the suggested queries, they received a lot of genealogical inquiries for baptism and marriage certificates.

I composed a note to the archivist, explaining that I was a family historian, doing work on priests within the family. All technically true, only a lie through omission. I asked for any papers or work from the three brothers, Fathers Fran, Bob and Joe. Finally, I asked for employment records. Within a few days, I received a brief reply. It included a listing of dates and parishes, and reassurance that there were no further papers on any of the three. I noted the birth and death dates, sites of education and ordination, and a listing of work assignments. I highlighted the key year of Kathleen's birth, 1951.

Once I had a list of locations, I tried to cross-reference them with Ginny's name. I called the parishes of note, one by one. My standard question was: "I'm looking to see whether Ginny Roethle was employed there as a housekeeper in the 1950's?" The response was a variant of stunned silence to flat "no." I was reaching modern parish secretaries, people concerned with the day-to-day operations of their parishes. They had neither the time nor the inclination to go delving into records from 60 years ago, if such records were even available in the first place. If anyone in a parish had memory or record of the historical housekeepers of a parish, these people were likely aging quietly at home, not working answering phones and administering church affairs.

I've since learned that parish housekeepers were not actually church employees. They were usually contracted by the priest himself, in a private arrangement. They were generally not paid, doing the work in exchange for room and board. Sometimes a priest's housekeeper travelled with him from parish to parish, acting as a gatekeeper and helpmate of sorts. Housekeepers were neither employees nor wives, but occupied a nebulous place somewhere in between—a place with no employment records.

* * *

Around the same time that I reached a dead end on the Paul McArdle and housekeeper lines of inquiry, I decided to go ahead and submit my DNA to 23andme. Despite all of the historic leads that Kathleen, Liz, and I unearthed, none were drawing us closer to the truth. It was rapidly becoming apparent that we would have to rely almost wholly on the clues buried in Kathleen's DNA. I knew how I was related to all of the potential fathers, so a comparison with my DNA would be as good a starting place as any. In retrospect, I am not sure why it took me so long to have my spit analyzed, but I have a few theories.

I ignorantly viewed DNA analyzing services as the "lazy person's" way of doing genealogy. For so many years, family histories were safeguarded by people like me—those of us who maintained and studied family trees, who visited cemeteries for fun, who saved all the newspaper clippings and funeral cards. If a relative needed information on family history, they had to contact the family archivist. I enjoyed being the boss of all that information. My family didn't nickname me "The General" for nothing. A teensy bit of me resented the fact that 23andme made family research too easy and available to the masses.

This concern was unfounded. Services such as 23andme will never wholly replace true genealogical research. The sites are mostly good for a "Gee Whiz!" type of research, calculating a person's ethnic percentages and whatnot. That and turning up relatives—up to 1,000 in Kathleen's case. For most people, after you exchange a few "huh, how are we related?" type messages with the people on your list, the conversation stalls. Now, if one of the people happens to be a family historian, the digging may go deeper. I decided to think of the sites as a way to hook people into the field of family history—a genealogy sampler platter. Maybe 23andme would introduce me to some new relatives that would be interested in my archives. Maybe I would meet someone who could add to my collection. Either way, I still needed to maintain an office full of newspaper clippings and ephemera. Take that, 23andme! You'll never rob me of my extensive collection of obituaries.

Finally, I think that on a subconscious level, I didn't want to open any doors linking Kathleen too closely to me, thereby pointing to Father Ed as her biologic father. But by this point in the search, I was pretty darn sure that Father Ed wasn't her father. But I wasn't completely certain—maybe even less so than when Father Raymond Parr was still on the list. I accepted that Kathleen's priest-father was hanging out somewhere in my Bier family tree, and my DNA was our best bet at zeroing in on that person. On a side note, I was surprised that no Biers showed up on her 23andme report, that not one of the hundreds of us jumped on the DNA analysis bandwagon. There were certainly enough of them floating around, but zero in the world of 23andme.

I ordered the kit, and the entire process was simple. A neat little package arrived, along with clear instructions. I had to fast for 30 minutes before filling up a tube with a generous sample of saliva. I spent about an hour slowly spitting into the tube. My kids thought it was pretty hilarious. The sample went into a pre-labelled box for mailing, and I registered a unique code online to create my profile. Then I waited. It took me longer than usual to get my results, as my first sample was rejected. Louise suggested that I should fast for a longer period prior to spitting to ensure a more concentrated sample, which I did with my second attempt a few weeks later. And then I waited some more.

I hoped to have my results in time for the Nashville genetics summit. In the meantime, I reviewed the data that we did have and attempted to make sense of it on my own—without Louise. While I cautioned Kathleen that we couldn't draw any conclusions on the 23andme relationship data just yet, I went ahead and began to do so anyway. Now, it was a matter of waiting for my DNA results and continuing to organize my thinking in an ever-expanding series of spreadsheets. I added this information to the table I'd constructed on the potential fathers' whereabouts, and clicked with pleasure between my ever-expanding cache of data, leads, and ideas.

Casebook summary

•Father Paul McArdle did not attend school at St. Francis Seminary. He never worked in Wisconsin.
oMost likely Kathleen's priest-father did not know Father Paul at all before leaving Ginny in his care.
•Need to get more Bier DNA to help narrow the field. (Mine and others').

Potential Fathers

Edward Bier   Francis Bier
Robert Gassert   Charles Bier
Robert Bier   Raymond Parr
Joseph Bier

Chapter Eleven
Henry

I was riding high on the wave of fruitful research. Things were falling into place nicely. I had basic information on all the potential priests. I eliminated two. I soon would have further genetic information and a plan to interpret it. We still didn't have a father identified, but we were rapidly closing in.

One early summer afternoon, when the girls were both outside, playing with friends, I logged into my genealogy software and updated both it and my private Ancestry.com tree. I had a warm glow of satisfaction as I extended the Bier family line back to Adalbert and, once and for all, created the correct connections with the previously untethered Parr relatives. I updated Kathleen on my successful solution to the Bier-Parr mystery, and my doubts that Father Raymond Parr was her father.

From: Me
To: Kathleen LeFranc

Since you sent me your 23andme login information, I'm going to send you my login for Ancestry; you can go through my family tree on there. Not to sound like a know - it - all, but I'm pretty sure that, at this point in time, I know the most about the Valentine Bier family of anyone alive, at least that I've found! I've kept my tree private because I have a lot of notes in there that aren't necessarily verified and are just word of mouth memories. I like those kinds of things, but I've gotten burned in the past with relatives finding my reminiscences and scolding me for sharing "hearsay." So, private it is.

I researched Fr. Raymond Parr at Alverno College in Milwaukee. He sounds like an amazing man, but I don't think he likely crossed paths with Virginia. I went to St. Francis Seminary to see if Paul McArdle spent any time EVER there; again, he wasn't in the records. So, back to the DNA we go. That's what spurred me on to submit my DNA to 23andme and it's driving me nuts that they can't complete my sample [My samples were rejected twice for unclear technical reasons. Bad spit or something, I guess]!!!

While I waited for my 23andme sample to be processed, I planned out my next steps. I needed to complete timelines for all the potential priests. To do this, I planned further on the ground research and more delving into online databases. In addition, I finalized my travel arrangements to meet with Louise, and that would take care of tackling things from the purely genetics angle. Things were clicking along in the well-ordered manner to which I was accustomed. Not surprisingly, my well-ordered plans were rapidly upended.

From: Kathleen LeFranc
To: Me

Dear Angela,
I just received notification from 23andme that I had new relatives. When I signed in, it actually says that I have a brother!! Henry Fetta. I really need help trying to figure this out. He appears to be a full brother and he's related to everyone I am. Have you heard of this name? This just keeps getting crazier. It looks like he's four years younger than me and grew up in the same area I did. He even went to the all-boys Catholic school that was associated with my all girls Catholic school!!
You still have my password, correct?
I am sure you are busy, but definitely appreciate your help.
Kathleen

Before I even bothered checking to confirm her statement, I wrote back. I needed her to know how jaw-droppingly stunning this news was to me.

From: Me
To: Kathleen LeFranc

Holy crap!!!! Full sibling????? This is crazy.
AB

Then, I logged onto Kathleen's 23andme account. There, up at the top, ahead of her own son, was a man with whom Kathleen shared 50% of her DNA: Henry Fetta. I paused to consider the significance of this finding, and it floored me. This meant that Ginny and the priest had not just one, but two children over a span of years—and gave both up for adoption. Did this make the whole tricky story better or worse? Either way, all my carefully laid plans and earth-shattering discoveries were quickly relegated to the backseat. Anything involving the words "Adalbert" or "Parr" paled in comparison to this new word: "Henry."

Henry was the first to make contact. Kathleen wrote a brief biography and included it in her public 23andMe profile.

> I was adopted when I was two weeks old in Chicago Illinois. I know that my mother came from Wisconsin and went to Chicago to have me so no one would know she was pregnant. She supposedly had a relative, an uncle who was a priest who brought her to a Catholic parish in Chicago where she stayed with the parishioner until she gave birth. The state of Illinois opened up my files and has tried to find my family but there is a possibility all the information on my birth certificate is false. They recommended I join these DNA websites in hopes of finding people I'm related to and it looks like I actually have! I am hoping we can all connect.

This brief description was the first hint to Henry that his story was far more complex than he might have imagined. He wrote back, and Kathleen shared Henry Fetta's first correspondence with me.

From: Kathleen LeFranc

"Hi, Kathleen, our stories are incredibly similar. I was born on April 27, 1957, and adopted at six weeks from Catholic Charities orphanage in Chicago. Our mother's name on my birth certificate is Betty Rohner and I have her signature. She said she was from Kansasville, WI. Both her name and hometown are assumed to be falsified. I was born in Loretto Hospital, not too far from Trinity and as fate would have it, I went to Fenwick. I grew up in Clarendon Hills, went to Notre Dame grammar school, and now live in Northbrook, IL. I would be happy to share contact information so we can connect. Henry"

Sooo! Virginia used the name Betty at first when she was staying at the home in Evanston before I was born. Rohner is the last name she said belonged to my father. She called him Jerome Leo Rohner. [Kathleen's birth certificate uses the names Elizabeth Louise Becker and Jerome Leo Rohner]. I'm overwhelmed that whoever the father is....they both, four years later, did the same thing over again. Who does that? Say they were in love and we know that love was forbidden ...but why have two children and give them both up? Now I have to wonder if Father Paul was involved again with setting this adoption up. I've responded to Henry, but it looks like he doesn't know any more than what I did. Another family member. I can't wait till you get your DNA results!
I'm coming to Chicago mid-July to spend the week with my sister. I hope we will have the opportunity to meet. Looks like maybe Henry will want to join me.
Love, Kathleen

In a stroke of coincidence, Henry and Kathleen "met" each other on the anniversary of Ginny's death, May 31, 2018—17 years after their biological mother died. Kathleen immediately felt that the existence of a brother made her birth story more okay, somehow. She reasoned that if her parents stayed together for at least five years, there must have been some degree of affection in the relationship.

The nature of Ginny's and the priest's relationship was something that I struggled with from the beginning. When I first heard of the mystery and looked into my great-uncle, Father Ed, as a potential father, I tried to rationalize things. I reasoned that since Ginny was 19 and technically an adult when Kathleen was born, it couldn't have been a truly abusive relationship—right? Assuming no actual physical force was involved, it must have been a relationship of equals—right? But I always came back to the fact that a priest automatically had a position of power, especially to a girl raised in a devout, Roman Catholic family. The existence of Henry reframed the equation once again. A relationship of over five years suggested far more parity than I previously calculated—right?

Not that the elephant in the room up and vanished, though. "Priest" and "dad" aren't two words that usually go hand in hand. Kathleen grappled with the uncomfortable pairing for years. To Henry, the unbelievable truth was brand new. He was still at the very beginning of his journey of discovery when Kathleen accidentally let slip about the "priest / housekeeper thing" and felt badly—it was all still very raw for Henry. In retrospect, Kathleen regretted sharing the details of their birth history with Henry as quickly as she did. She worried that she unloaded too much on him.

From: Kathleen LeFranc
Fwd: Henry Fetta
To: Me

Hi, Kathleen,
Thank you for sharing our biological mother and father's story; the condensed version is simply incredible and my head is still spinning. You have done an amazing amount of research over the past ten years and have learned so much. I am trying to absorb that our biological mother studied to become a nun and reached the novice level, realized it wasn't for her and moved on, went to work with priests and became pregnant by one of them who is our biological father. And, as you said, they somehow stayed together over a four-year period, had two

children and gave both of us up for adoption. Wow! As I write this, I realize how unbelievable this is and how life takes so many twists and turns.

Here is what I know, which is very little, compared to the information you have gathered. I hired a research firm three years ago called Omnitrace out of Florida to help me, but they ran into a brick wall when they realized that the information on my birth certificate was falsified. They did a lot of research on the Rohner name around Kansasville, WI and came up with nothing. I then went through Catholic Charities and they only gave me non-identifying information. Here is how they described our mother in 1957: "24 years old, single, white and of German heritage. She reported that her mother and father were both of German heritage. She said she was Roman Catholic and it was documented that she was born in another Midwestern state. She was described as 5 feet, 2 1/2 inches with blue eyes, dark blonde hair and fair skin and typically weighed 105 pounds. She said her interests were bowling and swimming. She said she was the sixth child with a total of eight in the family, having five brothers and two sisters.

And this is how our mother described our father in 1957: "24 years old, single, white and of German heritage. He was 5 feet, 10 inches with blue eyes, blonde hair and a fair complexion and weighed 185 pounds." According to their records, she did not name my birth father but reported that he was a high school graduate and a salesman.

As you said, we have lots to catch up on. I have a couple of questions for you: 1) do you know if either or both of our biological parents are alive? My mother and father have both passed away, my mother in 2004 and my father in 2011. I could not have been blessed with more loving and caring parents and I have one sister who was also adopted from Catholic Charities and born in 1959. 2) You mentioned that you believe our mother's name was Virginia Roethle; how were you able to find that? Does a family of 8 children with 3 girls and 5 boys match your information? [Both this and Ginny's physical description match with what we knew of her.] 3) We have lived in Northbrook for 19 years and I am thinking we may know the person whom you will be visiting; please pass along if you are ok with sharing.

I would enjoy speaking by phone when convenient for you, my cell is xxx-xxx-xxxx. It would also be terrific to get together when you visit in July; for you to know someone in Northbrook and to be visiting them soon is amazing and a gift.

Sincerely, Henry

Henry seemed so formal! By this point, several months into our intense correspondence, I felt comfortable with Kathleen. Our communications were often brief, filled with abbreviations, typos, and emojis. By comparison, Henry seemed quite serious. What was he like? What would he think of the direction that we were taking our inquiries? Would he approve?

Henry's question about whether either of their parents were still alive broke my heart. It jerked me back to the reality that what I was involved in was more than just a fascinating mystery. It was more than a chance to put all my years of genealogical research to actual use. It was two people's lives. Actually, it was four people's lives: Kathleen, Henry, their father, and Ginny. The implications of what we were uncovering were becoming quite real.

Was it wrong that I enjoyed the search? This made me feel decidedly uncomfortable, and I mentally promised to always check in with Kathleen and Henry before I pursued anything. I reasoned that, as long as I was still being useful, I could justify my presence in their story. Besides, I still belonged in the mystery because I had some skin in the game, my own DNA. I hoped that the results would arrive soon. With a reunion date set for a little less than a month away, I had a deadline. I needed to narrow the list of potential fathers significantly and arrive with something conclusive to share. Unfortunately, the Nashville genetics summit was going to occur after the Henry/Kathleen/Roethle

Reunion. I had a little over a month to wait. In the meantime, I still had my to-do list and traditional genealogy leads to pursue.

There was one important bit of information that Henry provided that significantly advanced my knowledge. He was born in 1955. Kathleen was born in 1952, so Ginny and the priest must have been together from 1951-1955, at the bare minimum. Henry's birthdate allowed me to publicly and officially cross Father Raymond Parr off the list.

Casebook summary

•Ginny and the priest had two children together: Kathleen and Henry

•Ginny and the priest were together from 1950 through at least 1955

oFather Raymond Parr can be officially excluded, having begun residing at Alverno College in 1953

<u>Potential Fathers</u>

Edward Bier   Francis Bier
Robert Gassert   ~~Charles Bier~~
Robert Bier   ~~Raymond Parr~~
Joseph Bier

Chapter Twelve
Marquette

The arrival of Henry on the scene threw me into a tailspin. I felt a new sense of urgency to solve the mystery. Henry and Kathleen would meet for the first time in a few short weeks, and I was invited. I needed to justify my presence there with some information of value. After receiving Henry's letter, my hamster wheel brain spun late into the night. In addition to his very existence, Henry provided some new useful details. He had a copy of his mother's signature, written in her own hand—the most tangible link to Ginny yet. Then there were his birth records. Perhaps because he was adopted through a Catholic orphanage rather than privately, there were a few more traces of the truth in his records. Ginny's residence was listed as Kansasville, Wisconsin. A quick review of my priest information did not reveal any of them ever holding a post in Kansasville. No dice there.

Perhaps more important was the identifying information on his birth certificate. The description of Ginny's appearance and family background meshed with what we already knew of her. Could the description of their father be accurate as well? Obviously not entirely, given that his job was listed as "salesman," unless one considered priests "salesmen for God," which was a bit too metaphorical even for me. Ginny used the pseudonym "Betty Rohner" on Henry's birth certificate. The names on Kathleen's were "Elizabeth Becker" and "Jerome Leo Rohner." Hmmm. Betty could be a nickname for Elizabeth. And Rohner was used twice. There had to be something there. I stayed up way too late that night, going down rabbit holes on the internet in search of a connection to the name Rohner.

From: Me
To: Kathleen LeFranc

CC: Louise Bier

I didn't get much sleep last night as I sleuthed online. Louise is currently on a camping trip with our mother and aunts and "off the grid," so I'm anxiously awaiting her return and thoughts. Here are some things I put together:

The names Betty Rohner and Jerome Leo Rohner. Jerome and Leo are most likely taken from her father and brothers' names, don't you think? But what "Rohner" which she used twice? Rohner was the name of a famous German Jesuit theologian of the time, perhaps it's a tribute to that? There was a Father Theodore Rohner in Wisconsin, but I think he would have been quite old, comparatively. And besides, Kathleen already eliminated him. And I don't think he's related to the Parrs. Interestingly, however, the 1910 census shows that Father Theodore Rohner and Father Robert Bier worked at the same parish. This may be a red herring, but seems worth tracking down. I don't think that Father Robert Bier's DNA works to explain Kathleen's Parr connections, though. Louise, can you check this? This would be Robert Bier, son of Frank and Mary Bier (NOT the Mary that married a Parr). Of note, he was known to be an alcoholic and may not have made the best decisions. I'll continue to research Theodore Rohner, just to make sure he's not in the greater tree somewhere.

Where was Virginia from 1950-1955? This seems to be so vital to the whole thing! I can find her in the 1940 census, but I can't find a trace of her again until she dies in Oconomowoc. Kathleen, do you think Liz might be helpful here? Any letters with postmarks from Virginia? Labeled photos?
AB

My sister, Louise was, indeed, away. She joined up with my mom and two aunts for a camping trip that occurred annually for the past twenty years or so. Even when I was able to reach her several days later, she said that she simply didn't have the bandwidth to deal with these questions in the setting of her actual daily life. In addition to administering a multi-million-dollar NIH grant for Columbia University, she and her husband were helping her mother-in-law deal with declining health issues related to brain cancer. She was too busy to run numbers until we had that 48 hours in Nashville. Kathleen, however, was already several steps—actually laps—ahead of me in terms of my other questions. She and Liz addressed them years ago.

From: Kathleen LeFranc
To: Me
Angela,
Thanks so much for all the research and thoughts. . .
So, on my birth certificate, my mother said her name was Elizabeth Louise Becker and my father's name was Jerome Leo Rohner. Henry said his mother said her name was Betty Rohner. Yes, I believe she made up the names Jerome and Leo from her brother and her father. At least, it sure appears that way. I have been tracking the name Rohner since I was a child and it is nearly impossible to figure that out. I know when my cousin, Barb Surwillo, from the Roethle side (we share the same great grandfather), took me to the family graves, I saw Becker in there and also Rohner....so there have to be some in that area. I did look up Fr. Theodore Rohner. He's significantly older than Virginia....however, we shouldn't toss anything out. I know when I was in my 30s, I researched a Fr Rohner and saw that he had one niece whose last name was also Rohner. I searched her out, thinking she was my mother, and brought a picture to Mrs. Brummel to identify. But Mrs. Brummel said absolutely not. [Recall that Mrs. Brummel later positively identified Ginny's picture]. She passed away quite a while ago . . . Liz has helped immensely and I'm sure would love to help with anything else. There just isn't much of anything on Virginia. Liz sent me one picture. She thought that she spent most of her life back at home. However now we know she managed to get pregnant again and went back to Chicago to hide the second one too! Really feels like we're writing a British mystery or something.
Onward!
Kathleen

I was impressed with Kathleen's optimism and vigor. This search must have been taxing, but she seemingly never allowed these feelings to sneak into her correspondence. And so much for my grand schemes of tracking down her father through the sham names on the birth certificates. Jerome and Leo were Ginny's father and brother. Elizabeth was her grandmother. And Rohner? We may never know. After all, Ginny Roethle lied to bury the truth, not to leave behind tantalizing and solvable clues.

I was so disappointed. I really thought that I was on to something, that I might be able to provide a breakthrough. To soothe my injured pride, I again focused on the upcoming Nashville DNA summit, and repeatedly checked 23andme for my results like it was my part-time job.

From: Me
To: Kathleen LeFranc
Louise and I are meeting in mid-July, when my girls are away at summer camp. I wish this were purely from a philanthropic drive, but really, we both are just determined that the answer is somewhere in the data. Also, when you said this sounds like a British mystery, I couldn't agree more. And I think we need to write it! But we need to I.D. your father first!
I'm anxious to see OUR degree of relatedness.
Henry's letter is amazing. Now you, maybe? know your father's year of birth? 1932-33? But who knows what is accurate...except for the genes They don't lie?

AB

From: Kathleen LeFranc
To: Me
You'll have to come visit California. My sister arrives from Chicago tomorrow. I'm hoping there will be no delays at the airport. Glad to hear the girls are dancers! I was also. It's so much fun!

Kathleen had one sister and two brothers. Kathleen and one of the brothers were adopted, and her sister, Molly, and her other brother were biological children of the McHughs. Kathleen and Molly were close and exchanged frequent visits. I imagined that their relationship was sort of like Louise's and mine—one sister in the Midwest and the other transplanted to a coast, counting the days between visits, and relying on phone calls to shrink the distance forced upon us by adult life.

* * *

While I waited for my visit with Louise, I set about putting my genealogical facts in presentable order for the Roethle Reunion. I constructed simplified family trees to share. I went through my data and checked for accuracy and readability. One glaring absence was information on Father Bob Gassert, one of the potential priests. I hadn't pursued this angle—the one of Father Bob being their father—with a great deal of vigor. There were lots of records of Father Bob in the files that my grandma left me. Why? Because, like Father Ed, this relative held a place of honor in the family's collective memory. He was a scholar, a Jesuit, who rose to dean level at Marquette University. And he was something of a boyish dreamboat. None of these things precluded him from secretly fathering children, though. It was time to bite the bullet and nail down a timeline for Father Bob. This required another field trip, this one to Marquette University.

On that summer day, I had a babysitter arranged for the girls while I got my hair done and then visited the Marquette Archives. I never visited this part of the campus before, but I corresponded with the archivist a few years back. Father Bob Gassert had a long career at Marquette, and the University Archives maintained files on him. Father Bob wrote a eulogy for his Aunt Rosalie (Roethle) Bier, my great-grandmother, which I obtained and added to my own archives. In addition, he spoke at celebrations for several of his priest relatives, including his uncle, Father Charles Bier and his cousin, Father Joseph Bier. His observations made colorful additions to my genealogical cache. It would be interesting to see what other treasures were hiding in

Marquette's archival record of Father Bob. A trace of Ginny Roethle, perhaps?

After my stylist finished working miracles with my rapidly-graying hair, I drove down Wisconsin Avenue toward Marquette. Wisconsin Avenue is the historic main street of Milwaukee. It used to be called Grand Avenue, and, at one time, was lined with the mansions of the beer barons that helped build the city. Wisconsin Avenue stretches west from Lake Michigan, snaking through high rise office buildings, past the main branch of the public library, across an interstate, and eventually bisecting the Marquette campus. During the summer, it can be easy to miss the transition from city to campus. During the school year, the crosswalks are lined with students in Marquette blue and gold streaming between classes, crossing the busy thoroughfare with the blissful invulnerability of youth. The school is a Catholic Jesuit one, and the large church on campus is called Gesu. The library building was located several doors down from this hulking a monster of a gray stone building.

I applied to Marquette for college but didn't seriously consider it. Back then, Milwaukee was a Big City, overwhelming to my country girl eyes. It felt the same when I toured the Marquette campus my senior year of high school. They offered me a very nice scholarship, but I just wasn't ready for the concrete urbanity of it all; I ultimately declined their offer of admission and scholarship. Now, I saw the campus with a much more acclimated eye. Marquette did their best to give it a collegiate feel, with unions and green spaces. But ultimately, the campus rubbed shoulders with a major highway interchange, and neighborhoods that became run down as the cycle of poverty shifted to Milwaukee's north side.

Father Bob Gassert grew up in one of those north side neighborhoods, about two miles from the Marquette campus, back in the day when those bungalows housed middle class families. Relatives spoke of Father Bob's devotion to his parents, especially his mother, Emily. Emily was the second youngest of the Valentine Ten, and the second of the Janesville Biers to permanently relocate more than a stone's throw from the farm. Emily Bier became Emily Gassert and raised a family of five in Milwaukee, eventually presiding over a clan that grew to 28 grandchildren—the most of any of the Valentine Ten. She was, by all accounts, a kind, benign presence. Biers of my father's generation recall driving the then-elderly Valentine Ten siblings over to visit their sister, "Em," for the day. Likewise, Emily's city kids would spend a week or two at the Bier home farm every summer. My mission today was to determine what Bob Gassert was getting up to between growing up in Milwaukee and spending his entire career at Marquette University.

I drove to visitor parking, consulted a campus map, and walked the few short blocks to Raynor Library. My appointment was in the archives. That department was tucked way off the beaten track, on the third floor. The entrance to the large library was security controlled, and I had to sign in and show identification. I took the elevator to the third floor and entered the archives. I was greeted by a no-nonsense, steel-gray haired woman. Any attempts at chatty repartee were quickly shut down. She listed off the few items allowed inside and directed me to lockers to deposit all of my contraband.

The head archivist emerged from a back office, pushing a rolling cart with four large storage boxes. I was pleased to see that they were of similar design and quality to those that I purchased for my own home archives. I was trying to run a reputable operation out of my home office, after all. The young woman gave me permission to photograph documents of interest and reassured me that I didn't need to wear protective cotton gloves. Then she left me to it—under the watchful, wary eye of the receptionist. I couldn't help but think back to Alverno's casual, cozy library in comparison .

The Raynor Library was remarkably quiet, given the urban traffic that streamed by just outside the windows. There were two other researchers working at tables, and we fastidiously minded our own business. I was there to review only a portion of the collected files of Father Robert Gassert. I requested his personal correspondence and miscellaneous personal papers. I didn't request his speeches and homilies, or his scholarly works. These would have been of genealogical interest. However, on that afternoon, I approached his files as part of the Kathleen Mystery, not as a straight-up genealogist. I probably should have called it the Kathleen & Henry mystery at this point, but old habits die hard.

As I mentioned, I was already all but certain that Father Bob Gassert wasn't their father. He just seemed too darn squeaky clean and GOOD. Truly a mama's boy, by all reports. In fact, Father Bob reportedly turned down career-advancing promotions outside of Marquette because he didn't want to move far from his mother. Even if he wasn't Kathleen and Henry's father, though, Father Bob's extensive files could still be of use. I planned to fill in the gaps in his educational chronology. I also wanted to see if any of his correspondence hinted at a scandal in the larger family circle.

I spent about three hours in the archives. I quickly filled in his educational history: undergrad at St. Louis University, brief teaching and coaching stint at an all-boys school in northern Wisconsin. Then Jesuit theological training at St. Mary's College in Kansas, and Gregorian University in Rome. He was at the last two institutions during the critical 1951-1955 stretch, and nowhere near Wisconsin. Father Bob was quickly and officially off the list, Rome being pretty darn far from Wisconsin.

I didn't find any smoking guns in the form of family gossip either. Despite this, I was thrilled by those files. They included a collection of letters that Bob Gassert sent to his older brother stationed in California in World War Two. There were the letters that he sent back home to his mom and dad between the 1940s through the 1970s. They were full of the banal details that make old letters and diaries so valuable. I was reminded of the importance of staying faithful to my daily journal writing.

It was a fun afternoon, if not necessarily earth-shattering. I could have spent all day there, picking the files apart. When I returned home, I was bombarded by real life. The girls wondered where I had been. By this point, the answer "working on the genealogy mystery" was answer enough. I mentioned that I also had my hair done, and my twelve-year-old asked whether I intentionally colored my hair more gray. Sigh. I explained the concept of cool blonde, updated my priest timelines, and got to work preparing dinner.

Casebook summary

- Father Bob Gassert is not Kathleen's father
  o He was out of the state and country at the time of her conception and birth
- How much longer can it possibly take to process my DNA????

<u>Potential Fathers</u>

Edward Bier   Francis Bier
~~Robert Gassert~~   ~~Charles Bier~~
Robert Bier   ~~Raymond Parr~~
Joseph Bier

Father Robert Gassert, first mass

Father Robert G. Gassert
of the Society of Jesus
1921-1993

Died peacefully in the Lord
June 17, 1993

Father Bob Gassert's funeral program. He died of cancer and was quite thin toward the end of his life. I love that this photo captures his optimistic, joyful persona in the face of this.

The surviving five of the Valentine Ten in the late 1960s. Back row: Father Charles Bier, Edward Bier (my great-grandfather). Front row: Emily (Bier) Gassert (Father Bob's mother), Frances (Bier) Hanauska, Amalia (Bier) Bott (Father Charles' longtime housekeeper).

Chapter Thirteen
Results

The Fourth of July came and went. The girls spent a week in New York with Aunt Louise at what we called "City Camp," learning urban survival skills. Jimmy and I enjoyed a dress rehearsal of empty nesting and realized that we still appreciated each other's company. I checked in on the Kathleen and Henry mystery frequently, refreshing my email inbox and the 23andme homepage.

And one day, boom. There it was, an email telling me that my results were in. I quickly logged onto my 23andme account, clicked past the information on my ethnic constitution (mostly German, French, and Lithuanian—no news there) and genetic trait reports (I can likely smell asparagus odor in my urine—again, no news). Eventually, I found it: my DNA Relatives Report. In the entire summary of just under 1,000 people to whom I was somehow related, Kathleen was literally at the top, followed closely by Henry. We shared around 5.5% of our DNA. Using 23andme's algorithm, we were tagged as second cousins. I was far more related to them than I was to Liz. We were definitely on the right track by looking in the Bier family tree for their father.

From: Me
To: Kathleen LeFranc

I just got my profile, have to run, so barely have time to think about it, but I'm more closely related to you and Henry than I am to Liz. Your father is somewhere in my family tree.

Like the Lithuanian-ness and asparagus pee, this wasn't really news. It was the conclusion that we circled around all along. But it certainly was nice to have our assumptions confirmed. After all, I would have hated to start a whole 'nother list of potential priest fathers at this stage of the game. Kathleen and I furiously typed back and forth.

From: Kathleen LeFranc
To: Me
Omg!!!!!!!!!!!!!! Yeah for us!!!!

From: Me
To: Kathleen LeFranc
I know. I have to call Louise so she can recommend who else to test. I think my dad for sure!
AB

I immediately tried to use the new information to identify the Bier clan that included Kathleen and Henry. Could we conclude that Valentine was our most recent common ancestor? And if so, which one of the Valentine Ten was likely Kathleen's and Henry's paternal relative? I couldn't simply trust 23andme's suggestion of how I was related to Kathleen and Henry. In the 23andme algorithm's world, 5.5%=second cousin, but the algorithm couldn't possibly account for all of the complexities of our relationship. We already knew that I was also related to Kathleen and Henry through their mother. How much of our shared DNA was due to that relationship? Kathleen's enthusiasm, however, went immediately to 23andme's straight-forward, seductive deductions.

From: Kathleen LeFranc
To: Me
Okay, I am not an expert in any of this by any means, but it appears that you and I share the same grandfather/great-grandfather. You really need to have your dad spit ASAP! There's an extremely strong possibility he is my first cousin. . . Wild!!!!! ..... we just might be back to Father Ed! Holy guacamole! I do not want to say a thing about this to

anyone until you girls get this figured out, but please have your dad spit ASAP

After spending so much time untangling the branches of the tree, I knew that 23andme's interpretation of our results couldn't possibly account for the complexity. I also understood Kathleen's unbridled excitement. A simple solution dangled temptingly. 23andme says we're second cousins—so Father Ed is the only explanation! I hated to be a downer, but they don't call me "Old Wet Blanket Ang" for nothing.

From: Me
To: Kathleen LeFranc
Caveat... some degree of our relations is though through the Roethles, remember

From: Kathleen LeFranc
To: Me
Correct... but that should mirror Liz's relationship then, right? Okay.... make sure you check out Dennis Parr's DNA comparison. Pretty much seals the deal.... AHHHHHHHH.... get Louise on the phone! This would make Henry and me Biers and Roethles on both sides of the family. If this is true, this is a doozy to grasp.

I think that where Kathleen was getting hung up was seeing our relatedness as being an either / or phenomenon. That is, our degree of relatedness was due either to her mother or to her father. Kathleen assumed that all our relatedness in the 23andme report came from her father. I knew, however, that our relatedness was not an either / or situation, but rather a both / and situation. That is, our 23andme relatedness came from both her mother and her father. I ran my conclusion by Louise, and she agreed. We couldn't draw simple conclusions from 23andme's data. I threw another bucket of cold water in Kathleen's virtual direction.

From: Me

To: Kathleen LeFranc

She [Louise] is very measured in the interpretation of the results and isn't quite ready to draw conclusions. We both agree that we wish we could just devote 8 hours to this right now, but we're going to have to wait for the July conference. We promise to send frequent dispatches.

Basically, what we'll do is construct hypothetical scenarios for various "clans" of the tree, determine probability numbers, and then identify likely people in the branches to ask for samples to help narrow things down. It's going to be tricky, given the degree of inter-relatedness of all of the branches...

I told her that I'm halfway between your excitement and her measuredness, so I get the desire to just be done with it already! Sorry we're not quite ready to call it yet!

AB

I was starting to feel terribly guilty. All my recent messages to Kathleen were admonitions to calm down, and explanations of why her thinking was wrong. I hoped that she wasn't becoming annoyed and frustrated with me. I only felt worse when I wasn't able to convince my father to spit. I kept him apprised of progress in the case, and he welcomed information on new developments. However, he never met either Kathleen or Henry and didn't have adequate personal investment to overcome his natural skepticism at the entire field to DNA analysis, despite two of his daughters' professions. He didn't quite understand the whole thing. He wasn't ready to spit.

In retrospect, I don't know why I didn't consider asking either of his siblings to do so. Their DNA would have been just as useful in terms of including or excluding Father Ed. Maybe on some level, I wanted to be darn sure that I knew what the results would be before submitting. I still was protective of Father Ed's reputation. In medical school, I received good advice on ordering lab tests.

"Doctors," Dr. Sebastian would intone, "ordering tests is like picking your nose. It's OK to do it, but you better make sure you know what you're going to do with the results." Would that more people heeded that warning before spitting for 23andMe!

From: Me
To: Kathleen LeFranc

I talked to my dad this morning; he's not ready to spit, I'm sorry to say. . . He does have a lot of other first cousins, but I want to get my ducks in a bit more of a row before approaching them. As I mentioned when we first corresponded, Fr. Ed is a near saint-like figure for most of them. Realistically, I'll need my dad (one of the eldest cousins) on board first, I think. So, it'll happen eventually.

I hope you weren't hurt by my "wet blanket" response yesterday. I want to help you solve this too. I just feel like as we close in on the answer, knowing my people, this must be done delicately.

From: Kathleen LeFranc
To: Me

Angie,
I totally understand. Nobody wants to jump to any conclusions in a situation like this. We need to be positive. I do know you are my first cousin once removed, so whoever it is, they are very close to you as well as to me.
I did make a discovery today, researching through old Janesville Gazettes. There was an article about a Barbara McCue (Helen Bier's niece) getting married. Liz told me that Virginia was in her wedding party. Upon reading the article, it states that a Reverend Joseph V. Bier came from North Fond du Lac, Wisconsin, to read the nuptial mass for his cousin. Also coming from North Fond du Lac, Wisconsin, was Virginia Roethle. This puts up a red flag to me. Do you know anything about this priest? Since Liz mentioned this to me, I just sent her an email, asking if she knows anything about this priest. I'm not

137

mentioning anything to anybody about Father Ed until we are positive. But this other priest is a strong possibility. On Henry's adoption papers, Virginia named him Joseph. This article was written January 23, 1961, after both Henry and I were born.

Hmmmmmm

Love,

Kathleen

PS I might be groping here, but I don't want to hurt the family any more than you. It's worth checking out all possibilities

PS... The wedding was at St Mary's Church.

Kathleen was amazing! She got a lot further along with the three brother priests than I did. They continued to languish, relatively ignored, on my potential fathers list. I managed to find pictures and employment histories, but not much else. Here was an article that actually put Father Joseph Bier and Ginny together at an event—and possibly had them traveling into Janesville from the same city several hours away. I found a copy of the article and went over it with a fine-tooth comb. All out-of-town guests had their hometowns listed. Father Joseph Bier and Virginia Roethle are mentioned several paragraphs apart. You had to really be paying attention to notice that they both arrived from Fond du Lac.

From: Me
To: Kathleen LeFranc

Oh, good. I was worried I hurt your feelings.

Now, on to Father Joe. That is a tantalizing clue.

You'll notice that Frank and Mary (Klein) Bier had three sons who were priests. Here's what I have in my notes about Father Joe:

Ordained 6 June, 1936. Studied at Saint Francis Seminary (Milwaukee, WI). Assistant at St. Mary, Pewaukee '36-'37. St. Matthew, Milwaukee '37-'44. St. Kilian, Hartford '44-'45. St. Rita, West Allis '45-'51. Pastor at St. Francis Xavier, Brighton '51-'60. Presentation of the Blessed

Virgin Mary, Fond Du Lac, 1960-'67. St. James, Menomonee Falls '67. retired '68. Buried at St. Francis Xavier Cemetery in Brighton.

I find it interesting that he chose to be buried at St. Francis in Brighton rather than with his family.

Really, for me, what it comes down to is trying to figure out how much "relatedness" we can subtract out for us based on your mother, and then running hypotheticals for all of these priests and seeing who matches up the best. Then maybe finding likely test candidates in each of the Valentine Bier "clans" for DNA testing? Unfortunately, I don't really know anyone in the Frank Bier clan. I was contacted by someone through the blog and we exchanged a couple of emails, but that's about it. Same with the Emily Bier line [Father Robert Gassert's mother]. I feel like I need a little bit more "and based on the DNA, we're pretty sure that her dad is in your branch of the tree" beforehand. Does that seem reasonable?

I'm kind of liking Father Joe right now, especially that bit about traveling down together???

AB

From: Kathleen LeFranc
To: Me
Well, I don't think this is all as complicated as you're making it out to be. I pulled out all the family trees and opened up the 23andme explanation chart, along with doing the math on the segments of how we are related. When you have the time to spread it out, it will be pretty clear. But for now, we will definitely keep looking at any other first cousins. Whoever this priest is has to be very close to you and me in the bloodline. Father Joseph is a bit old, but try to figure out why Virginia would be up in North Fond du Lac. Mystery. Also, something came up in a blip I found on Reverend Theodore Rohner, residing in Fond du Lac. Now if Father Joseph knew him and Virginia knew him, that would be an easy name to put on a birth certificate that nobody

would trace. Just saying. Keeping all options open, but your DNA has really opened the door.

Another PS

You're not hurting my feelings. This has been a very difficult search emotionally for me. I really try to walk in other people's shoes, so I can only begin to imagine what this news could do to a lot of people. I know we are right there now. We will tread lightly and be absolutely positive.

While I was a little irritated by what I read as snippiness at the beginning, I was also touched by Kathleen's admission of her own vulnerability through the journey. That she was emotionally invested was not a surprise, but I sometimes forgot. Her email presence was so relentlessly upbeat and cheery.

While we waited for our meeting in a few short weeks, the railway train car of DNA analysis completely ran away at the LeFranc house. In sunny California, Kathleen's husband was deeply involved in the mystery as well. We never talked much about him, so I was surprised that he was working on the mystery so diligently. I was confused by his message. It laid out his analysis of our 23andme results and drew some conclusions, but I failed to follow his logic. The gist of his conclusions, though, was that the only explanation for Kathleen and my relatedness was that Father Ed Bier was her father. Not surprisingly, I disagreed.

Oh dear. I thought that I could dry out my wet blanket and put it away, but I needed Kathleen to keep an open mind for the time being. I could tell that her husband felt that I was failing to adequately consider Father Ed. Honestly, at that point, that ship had sailed. I made my peace with the facts of the case as they stood. I started to do some side reading on the phenomenon of children of priests and came to have a much more measured understanding. I really wasn't trying to stonewall them! Out of a sense of defending my academic honor, I made one last Hail Mary attempt at explaining my logic. And boy, was it pedantic. So pedantic, in fact, that a summary is better than the painful email itself.

How do we figure out how much of our relatedness comes from your dad? Is it

(total relatedness) - (mom relatedness) = (dad relatedness),

or is it a far trickier calculation due to the fact that your mom and dad were somehow related themselves? I suspect the latter.

The rest of the email was in simple English. . .

From: Me
To: Kathleen LeFranc

. . . I am literally just waiting until my meeting with Louise and her fancy geneticist programs to sort this all out. One way or another, we are related two ways, which is super cool, and both the Biers' and the Roethles' stories are yours to embrace!

xoxo

AB

As I thought through the calculations, something remarkable struck me. Kathleen and Henry were, most definitely, Biers two ways—through their mom and their dad. They had a double helping of Bier-ness. They were Bier-er than any of the Biers who already knew that they were Biers! What would all of those cousins scattered around southern Wisconsin make of that fact? The Bier-est Biers were essentially unwitting carriers of that legacy.

Casebook summary

•Kathleen & Henry's father is somewhere in the Valentine Bier descendent tree for sure

•90% certain that we are not related through Father Ed—but keep him on the list for now

oNashville Genetics Summit can't come soon enough!

•Why did Ginny and Father Joe both travel down from Fond du Lac to attend a wedding in Janesville?

Potential Fathers

Edward Bier (highly unlikely)   Francis Bier
~~Robert Gassert~~   ~~Charles Bier~~
Robert Bier   ~~Raymond Parr~~
Joseph Bier

Chapter Fourteen
Anticipation

In the weeks leading up to our meeting, I wanted to mend whatever rifts my emails created with Kathleen. I worried that the misunderstandings about my 23andme results soured an enjoyable friendship. I tried to be mindful of the fact that this was her and Henry's story. I wanted to continue to be a helper and supporter, not a naysayer or voyeur. As a token of goodwill, I sent her some pretty versions of Bier and Roethle family trees, complete with photos. That seemed to do the trick.

From: Kathleen LeFranc
To: Me
This is great! Thank you. I forwarded it to Henry who I will be talking to in a half hour. This is our second Saturday morning chat. What a strange and wonderful world we live in!

Although I had yet to communicate with Henry directly, Kathleen forwarded my messages to him, and vice versa. I enjoyed his thoughtful letters. They were quite different from mine—laced with sarcasm—and Kathleen's—laced with exclamation points and emojis. She sent Henry my most recent message with the trees, along with strings of our perusals.

From: Kathleen LeFranc
To: Me
Begin Fwd from: Henry Fetta
Kathleen,
Thank you so much for sharing this e-mail thread with me. It really helped get me up to speed on the linkages and latest thinking on our father. It also showed me how we are connected to such special people.

Not only have we found one another, this family is amazingly welcoming, caring and giving. We are blessed.

I look forward to building on the itinerary together. Lynn [Henry's wife] and I can meet earlier than 11, but that's up to you and Molly [Kathleen's sister] as you must travel further. I have this peaceful sense that we are going to meet some folks who knew our mother and family somewhere in and around Neosho during our journey. I do hope we can see the school our mother and her siblings attended. It's so nice of Angela and Louise to take up the DNA cause, how special.

At one point, I assumed that Henry's formal tone might hide criticism of our methods. As I read more of his missives, I realized that the formality was due to his extreme care with words. I always admired people who construct communications that aren't full of trip-ups. Being incapable of restrain, I often spend hours lying awake at night, reliving painful faux pas of the past. I looked forward to meeting this classy guy.

The Roethle Reunion, as I christened it, was planned around Kathleen's visit to the Midwest. She would stay with her sister in the Chicago area. Kathleen originally planned to travel alone; however, once Henry hit the scene, Kathleen's husband decided that he wanted to be there for the meeting of the siblings as well. Henry would come up to Ginny Roethle's hometown, along with his wife. We would meet at the home of Barb Surwillo, the archivist of the Roethle family. She was the first 23andme relative that Kathleen ever contacted, even before Liz, and was instrumental in identifying Ginny.

The intimate reunion grew rapidly in size and scope. Barb still lived in the general vicinity of the Roethle home village of Neosho. She planned informative stops at important Roethle landmarks. I wouldn't miss it for the world. I had "visit Roethle area" on my genealogy to-do list for quite some time. In return, I offered to arrange stops at important Bier landmarks. The day after, Henry and his wife invited everyone to their home north of Chicago for a barbecue. His kids would be there, too. I couldn't attend this bit of the weekend. However, I felt that this might be best. Given the frenetic pace of Saturday, Henry and Kathleen would need some time together to unpack and decompress.

While Barb, Kathleen, and I built out an ambitious itinerary, Henry continued to express a desire for meaning and connection. A brief sample from one of his thoughtful, lengthy notes to Kathleen captures where he was at:

From: Henry Fetta
To: Kathleen LeFranc, Me

For our trip . . . I would like to spend time understanding where the Roethle family lived, where they went to church, where they went to school, where they shopped, where they played outside of the farm, where the children were born. I want to walk a path that Virginia took sometime during her life and experience that with you. I am wondering if some folks in Neosho and/or the surrounding villages would remember the family and some members and have a story or two or three to share. It would be amazing to meet some locals who knew Leo, Helen [Ginny's parents] and the kids. I guess I'm saying I am happy to immerse ourselves in their community before spending a lot of time shuffling between sites but that may be the best approach to help fill in the story.

It is so nice of Barb and Angie to offer to host us; on the flip side, it would be great to eat at a local place where the family may have gone and take Barb to lunch or dinner. Just a thought.

One of the reasons I had yet to visit the Roethle area on my own was that there wasn't really a clear place *to* visit. The villages were villages in the truest sense of the word, a clustering of houses at a crossroads. Henry was a Chicago boy, unfamiliar with "middle of nowhere" Wisconsin, where you couldn't really just wander around and bump into people. Kathleen captured the reality of the situation well.

From: Kathleen LeFranc
To: Me

So cute that Henry wants to visit local restaurants. When I drove through Janesville a couple years ago, the Ponderosa steakhouse looked like the hotspot in town. I don't think that's quite what he had in mind!! Maybe there is a local pub where we could gather some of the family? Does that seem a ridiculous thought?

In the end, we decided to spend the morning and early afternoon in the Neosho area, and then make the drive to the Janesville area. Barb would plan the Neosho bit, and I would organize the Janesville bit—arrange for dinner somewhere, attempt to gain access to the Valentine Bier family farm, and possibly a visit to St. Mary's Church. Kathleen extended the invitation to several of her contacts from Janesville who would join us for the Janesville half of the day. I kept a running tally for dinner; it was rapidly growing into the teens. An important next step would be inviting my dad along. Kathleen wanted to meet him, and he was my ticket in with all the local Biers relations.

Finding a good local watering hole wasn't a problem. Since there weren't any historic restaurants in the Roethle villages, I arranged charm and ambience in the Bier area. My newfound cousins needed a true Bier baptism at a legitimate supper club. I made a reservation for 15 at my favorite, The Duck Inn. Then I started inviting locals. I wondered whether my father would be interested. He was so hesitant to submit a saliva sample. Was his hesitation more due to a suspicion of the technology and privacy concerns? Or was he holding a chip on his shoulder about Kathleen suspecting his beloved uncle, Father Ed? I suspected the former. I called my folks one Sunday a few weeks before the Roethle Reunion.

"Hey, Ang," my dad answered. "What's new?"

"Do you remember me telling you about Kathleen, and now Henry?"

"Yeah..."

"Kathleen is going to be in Chicago, visiting her family in a few weeks, and she's arranging a get-together to learn more about the Roethle family. She wanted to make sure that I invite you along."

"That'd be real interesting. I think I'm free that day. I'll have to check and get back to you. I locked myself out of the house and can't remember where we hid the key," he said. The man was not a fan of modern technology. "I'm waiting for Mom to get home to let me in. Okay if Mom comes along?"

"Sure. I figure she'll enjoy it just for the genealogy stuff. I think we're going to a couple of farms and a cemetery," I said.

"Neat."

"And then I was hoping to show them Eleanor's house, just to show them where the Biers started. We don't know which Bier priest was their father yet, but it for sure was one of them. Do you think that'd be okay?"

"I'm sure that would be fine. I'll check with her."

"I was thinking of seeing if anyone else from the Trip to the Homeland might want to come along too."

"Let me talk to a few people and get back to you. But it's a plan," Dad said.

I hung up, pleased that my dad sounded so interested in the process. When he was growing up, his family would have occasionally visited their Roethle great-aunts and uncles, and he always was up for a trip down memory lane.

Of course, Dad was able to arrange a visit to the Valentine Bier farm. In addition, one of his cousins was interested; this was one of Eleanor's daughters. She went on the Bier trip to the Homeland the previous summer, and I thoroughly infected her with the genealogy bug. I left the business of communicating with Auntie Eleanor, who was approaching 90, but still sharp as a tack, to my dad and her. In the meantime, I started putting together another spreadsheet to manage the day. This one, I titled, "Meeting."

* * *

While plans and itineraries were made, Kathleen's sleuthing continued. One interesting update was in regards to Jerome, Ginny's living brother with dementia. Jerome lived in a southern Wisconsin nursing home, near his son, Ted. Months previous, Kathleen contacted Ted and his wife to see if any of that family had any recollection of the time period around her birth. Did they know that Ginny had a child? Did they know which parish she was sent to? Did they know anything? Ted was reluctant to share information in the past, despite implying that he knew something. Now, Kathleen decided to let him know about Henry and see if that shook him loose a bit.

From: Kathleen LeFranc
To: Me
Angie,
Ted just responded to me on Facebook, congratulating me on having a brother, but is still saying he doesn't know anything. . .. I am hoping he will let me visit him on my way up to Wisconsin, along with meeting his father Jerome. . . .
Yikes,
Kathleen

I was amazed by Kathleen's fearlessness and determination. She received so many no's in this search, and yet she just kept plowing ahead. I would have been stymied, given my unhelpful habit of taking all no's as personal rebuffs. Was she for real? In a few short weeks, I would find out.

From: Me
To: Kathleen LeFranc

Hi, Kathleen,
Thanks for the update. It's good that Ted's responding to you. Fingers crossed for a face to face meeting with Jerome. He would have still been living at home around the time of your and Henry's births.
AB

To: Me
From: Kathleen LeFranc

Angie,

This is going to be delightful. My emotions are all over the place. . .
This is definitely a story to be told! Let us hope for a good finale.

It was around this time that I started keeping detailed notes on the
unfolding mystery. A story as intriguing as this surely needed to be
recorded and shared. And the twists and turns hadn't even yet begun in
earnest.

* * *

In the weeks leading up to the Roethle reunion, I prepared my data to
share with the group. I put together a huge family tree of the Valentine
Bier descendants, up to the generation of Ginny and all of the potential
priests. If I included my parents' and my generation, let alone our kids,
the several hundred individuals would have created something
hopelessly overwhelming and about six by eight feet. Even with those
more recent generations trimmed away, the information was swirlingly
dense   I did my best to create order out of the chaos. I color coded,
included pictures, and ended up with a visual aid that was taller than I
was, but only two sheets of paper wide. I took my creation to a copy
shop to be laminated, and the guy behind the counter was
dumbfounded.

"Are all these people your family?" he asked.

"Yup, one way or another," I answered.

I planned to bring along some pictures, including the large portrait
of the Roethle family that my daughter had spotted at the Honeypie
Cafe. I would, of course, bring my laptop, so that I could access my
digital archives. I lived for moments like these, when my tendency
toward organized hoarding paid off.

While I worked from my end, Kathleen continued her online
sleuthing. She focused on the potential priests that remained on the list,
especially the three priest brothers. Her Google skills were second to
none. I attempted similar searches, but was usually stymied by the
numerous ways that a priest's name might appear in print. For example,
Father Edward Bier could be: Father Edward Bier, Father Ed Bier,

Rev. Bier, Rev. E.J. Bier, Monsignor Bier, just to name a few. Kathleen's tenacity eventually paid off with some intriguing new information. She included me on a note to Henry.

From: Kathleen LeFranc
To: Henry Fetta
CC: Me

. . . found an interesting article from 1970 that I attached here. Looks like Father Joseph Bier, who would've been 23 years older than our mother, was a questionable character. He is the priest/cousin who, in 1961, came down from North Fond du Lac, where our mother also appeared to be living at that time, to officiate at the wedding of a cousin. Phew!!! Dizzying. Looks like we need to schedule another conversation! I'm really free anytime.
Hugs!!!

Kathleen
PS.... I'm counting the days till we meet!!!

I smiled at Kathleen's giddiness; that was a lot of exclamation points. I looked forward to meeting Henry and Kathleen both.

She found the article in a digitized newspaper archive, one of several commercially available to researchers. The article appeared in the 1970 *Waukesha Daily Freeman*, Waukesha is about 30 minutes west of Milwaukee, and 30 minutes southwest of the Roethle villages. The article reported on a lawsuit filed by a former rectory housekeeper—the housekeeper from the final pastoral assignment of Father Joseph Bier's career. She was *not* Ginny Roethle, or any other housekeeper I encountered previously. The housekeeper / plaintiff was noted to be a "divorcee and a beautician." She was not suing Father Bier, which was a small relief. Rather, she named the associate pastor and two other lay members of the parish in a case of libel and slander. While the plaintiff was noted to be a divorcee, the two parish leaders were described as "a businessman and village president."

According to the housekeeper, the associate pastor and these two men wrote, printed, and distributed pamphlets that were defamatory to her. The pamphlets alleged that she had an immoral relationship with the pastor of the church, Father Joseph Bier. She was then, "held . . . up to public ridicule, contempt, and hatred among members of the parish and in the Milwaukee Archdiocese." Father Joseph was neither a petitioner, nor a defendant in the lawsuit, but a material figure in the pamphlet's narrative. The article noted that "the Personnel Board of the Milwaukee Archdiocese said that Father Bier, 60, retired from the priesthood Nov. 2, 1968." The pamphlets were distributed in September and October of 1968.

This was yet another entry in my rapidly expanding catalogue of oddities in relationships between priests and their housekeepers. The facts of the case were insane. These parishioners and the junior priest must have felt so trapped by the rules of the day that they felt the only way to react to their suspicions was to publicly distribute pamphlets. And how did they distribute them—and to whom? Most likely, their goal was to have Father Bier disciplined, but the unfortunate housekeeper was swept up in the dragnet. She must have been enraged by this airing of her dirty laundry—true or not.

And what of Father Joseph Bier? In terms of fallout, all that I knew was that his 30+ year retirement commenced shortly after this article was published. Clearly, the two things were connected. Might he have done even worse? I checked into the possibility of further allegations having been raised against Father Joseph, and all the other priests on my list. Following years of scandal and litigation, the Archdiocese of Milwaukee maintains a public Database of Priests Accused of Sexual Abuse. It was a silly oversight that I didn't check it before. I was relieved to discover that no Bier or Parr priests appeared there.

What a mess. I was sucked into the drama, as Kathleen appeared to be. But what of sensitive Henry, so newly arrived on the scene? How was he handling this concerning piece of circumstantial evidence?

From: Kathleen LeFranc

151

To: Me
Fwd from: Henry Fetta
Hi, Kathleen,
Thanks for your note and for your summer wishes! You may have heard from Molly how dreary and rainy it's been in the Chicago area for the past month, but today is beautiful. Chicagoans appreciate nice weather because
they are so deprived of it :)

Thanks for the article on Fr. Joseph Bier, please remind me if he is Fr. Ed Bier's brother? Given the miraculous nature of events so far, I am confident that the story will unfold without DNA, but am happy to assist with the YDNA test if it's helpful [Kathleen encouraged Henry to have a particular type of DNA analysis completed]. Maybe we can talk about next steps when you're here. My son Mark is in FamilyTreeDNA and I have been trying to download the 23 and Me data into that site without success so far. I've followed the instructions, but still must be doing something wrong.

Mark works in San Jose' and we have not seen him since Christmas. He told us this week that he'd like to come home in July and would like to meet you, so he'll be here, along with two of our other children, their spouses and our grandchildren. Everyone is so excited to welcome you into our family.

Happy to talk anytime this week. People outside of the family whom I've shared our story with want it on Dateline :)
Hugs, Henry

I was chagrined by Henry's comments about the DNA analysis being immaterial. That was my biggest contribution! In reality, though, his summation was correct. Not for the metaphysical reasons that he suggested, but purely by virtue of the facts of the case. At this stage, with Father Ed still hanging on the list by a thread, three of the four remaining potential priest fathers on the list were brothers! Any DNA results would not—simply could not—differentiate between the three. If any of the three priest brothers were their father, Henry and Kathleen would appear identically related to anyone else we might test. They would be identically related to me, my dad, my cousin if ANY of the three were their father. The only relatives that would be more related to one brother than another would be an acknowledged child of one of the brothers, which we didn't have. We just had suspicions in the meantime.

Casebook summary

• Father Joseph Bier now has two pieces of highly suspicious circumstantial evidence pointing toward a possible connection to Ginny. And some evidence that he wasn't the most savory character.
    ○ Focus on his parishes in the 1950s to see if we can find ANY evidence of Ginny's presence there.
    ○ If we can place those two in the same parish, the case will be pretty much closed.
• The Nashville DNA Summit will be mainly confirmatory, I think.

Potential Fathers

Edward Bier (highly unlikely)
~~Robert Gassert~~
Robert Bier
*Joseph Bier
Francis Bier
~~Charles Bier~~
~~Raymond Parr~~

Three of the Roethle children: Leo Roethle is Ginny's father; he married Helen Bier. Clara Roethle remained unmarried and put out chocolate covered cherries at Christmas. Rosalia Roethle is my great-grandmother; she married Edward Bier.

Catholic Priest, 2 Other Men Named In Libel Suit Involving Morals Case

AN ASSOCIATE pastor of a Roman Catholic congregation in Lannon and two of his parishioners have been named defendants in a $1,525,000 libel action up to public ridicule, contempt and hatred among members of the parish and in the Milwaukee archdiocese.

The material was circulated among

The Personnel Board of the Milwaukee Archdiocese said this week that Father Bier, 60, retired from the priesthood Nov. 2, 1968, and is now living at Water-

Headline from the *Waukesha Daily Freeman article* about Father Joseph Bier's former housekeeper.

Chapter Fifteen
Meeting

I woke up on the morning of the Roethle Reunion, and it was beautiful—the kind of summer day that Wisconsinites live for, that sustains us through the winters that drag on and on. We dropped the girls at camp the day before, and my husband already left for work. Alone, I packed up my supplies and said goodbye to an empty house. The GPS predicted a 45-minute drive to Barb Surwillo's address, and I enjoyed every mile of it. Once I exited the freeway, I wound through the charming, varied kettles and moraines of Wisconsin's glaciated region. The route took me in a wide loop around the basilica on the hill named, appropriately enough, Holy Hill. As tour buses of retirees turned off to visit the picturesque shrine, I continued on to Barb's home. I felt a familiar burble of anxious anticipation as I turned into the unknown driveway, full of the unknown cars of known-yet-unknown people. A man who turned out to be Barb's husband puttered in the garage. He directed me into the house through the garage entrance, where I was deposited straight into the thick of things.

"Helloooooo..." I announced as I entered. A woman who could only be Kathleen was on the other side of the countertop, along with various other people milling about. She looked exactly like her picture and stood still in the center of the hive of activity, the emotional linchpin of the room. "Kathleen?" I asked, walking toward her with my arms outstretched.

"Hi, cousin!" she laughed and came in for a big hug. Kathleen was shorter than I was, thin, stylishly dressed in a button-down shirt and jeans with her dark hair pulled back into a sleek ponytail.

"I can't believe I'm finally meeting you for real!" I said with an uncontrollable grin.

"I know, oh, it's good to be here. Here, I brought something for you from California." She reached into a bag and pulled out a Starbucks mug with "California" printed on it.

"Perfect. I love coffee, as my girls would tell you."

"Well, that's good, cuz I'm a barista." How did I not know that she was a barista? Kathleen introduced me to her sister, Molly, who stood quietly in the background, and Barb, who was putting out pastries and drinks on the kitchen island. Henry and his wife were still en route.

Kathleen and Molly were clearly sisters, even though they looked absolutely nothing alike—Kathleen was dark complected and quite thin, while Molly had the typical coloring and full cheeks of an Irish lass. Their sisterhood shone in the way that they anticipated each other's movements, rather than in how they looked. Molly remained Kathleen's silent wingman the entire day, filming key moments and anticipating when she needed a break.

As I reflected on their dissimilar appearances, I realized that Kathleen didn't look anything like a stereotypical Bier. We tend to have broad features and farmers' builds. Glamorous, I know, but I'd long since come to accept what my mother awkwardly referred to as "The Bier barrel-chest." Kathleen was fine-featured, with a delicate jaw and hands. For half a beat, I wondered whether we'd gotten the whole "Bier priest" thing wrong.

Kathleen introduced me to Barb and their respective husbands.

"Thank you so much for including me in this, Barb," I said, shaking her hand.

"What a crazy thing, huh?" she replied. "I was telling Kathleen that people just can't believe this story when I tell them!" she said, offering me a bagel and coffee. I complimented her on her obviously recently remodeled kitchen.

"Yes, we just moved here about a year ago, and the kitchen definitely needed updating."

"Oh, aren't you from here originally?" I asked.

"I grew up here, but we moved away to raise our family and just moved back for retirement, to be near the grandkids."

"Now," I said, getting the genealogical juices flowing, "I think you are my father's second cousin, right? My second cousin, once removed, then?"

"That's right. My grandfather, Oscar Roethle, and your great-grandmother, Rosalie Roethle, were brother and sister," Barb said.

"Speaking of that family, I have an amazing picture to show you."

I went out to the car and came back, bearing the massive portrait of the Roethle family that I was gifted by the Milwaukee cafe. As Barb and I began identifying the individuals, the remainder of the group drifted over. I watched as Kathleen tried to make sense of it all.

"Now, that's Leo, right? He'd be my grandfather, Ginny's father?"

"Right," I replied. "And that one there is Rosalie, my great-grandmother. And that's Oscar, Barb's grandpa."

"Okay. And where does Frank Bier and his sons fit into this?"

"Well, they don't, at least not directly. These two," I pointed to Leo and Rosalie, "both married Biers."

Kathleen and Molly nodded, looking not at all convinced. The craziness of our being related two ways could not be overstated—or explained too many times.

"Right," said Barb. "I've arranged for us to go to the house where John and Katherine raised this family," she said, motioning to the studio portrait. "And then I got hold of the woman who lives in the house where Leo and Helen raised Ginny and her siblings. I never met her before, but she was real nice and said we could stop by after eleven." Barb ticked off itinerary stops on her fingers as she spoke.

"You mean the house where Ginny grew up?" Kathleen glanced up.

Barb nodded and continued. "Yup. It's one town over. There's a pub nearby where I thought we could stop for lunch. After that, I thought I'd take you to see where Ginny is buried south of here. She's not buried in the family plot. And then there's a ninety-year old former neighbor of the Roethles who remembers playing with them, going sledding with the kids on the hill by the river behind the house, who agreed to talk to you and Henry."

I started to worry that adding the Janesville leg onto the itinerary was going to be too much for one day. I asked Kathleen and Barb, but they both insisted it would be fine. I excused myself to see about moving our dinner reservations a bit later.

While I was on the phone, my parents arrived. After saying hello, Dad stopped with his hand on Kathleen's shoulder, a small smile on his face.

"Now, I don't want you to get too excited, but we pulled up alongside Henry, and he's waiting outside until we give him the all clear that it's time to come in."

"Oh my gosh, he's here?" Kathleen pressed her hands together.

It was agreed that Barb would go outside and show Henry in through the front door. Kathleen walked nervously alongside Molly to the small entry foyer. Molly got her phone ready, and the rest of us stood in the wings. My mom was across the foyer from me, just inside a hallway that led to bedrooms.

"Ready?" Barb stuck her head in the front door. When Kathleen nodded, she stepped back and Henry walked in, cradling four roses.

And how could we do anything but cry? Mom and I exchanged drippy smiles across the once-in-a-lifetime tableau. Henry and Kathleen said each other's names, stepped across the small foyer, and crushed each other in an embrace.

"I've never been the big sister before," Kathleen kept repeating.

When they finally were able to collect themselves, Henry presented Kathleen with the flowers. "I brought four roses. One for each of us, and one for our mother, and one for our father."

People talked excitedly over each other as introductions were made. Henry and Kathleen took each other in. Henry shook each of our hands, holding them a beat longer than what was typical, and expressed his gratitude through calm eye contact. I became a Henry fan immediately.

If Kathleen didn't look like a Bier, Henry was the prototype. From behind, he and my father could easily have been mistaken for each other, a fact that was highlighted by their outfits for the day. They both wore khaki shorts with a light blue polo tucked in, and sensible shoes with socks. And they both appeared to have the Bier barrel-chest.

The burbling group drifted into the roomy kitchen. I sat at the table with my parents, as Barb suggested that we go around the room and make introductions. I learned that Henry's wife, quietly his shadow, was named Lynn. Then, for the sake of getting everyone up to speed, Barb asked Kathleen to "briefly" tell her story. Kathleen condensed a lifetime of questions and searching into about 15 minutes. I leaned over to my mom.

"You following this?" I whispered. She doesn't have my dad's family tree committed to memory, despite being a natural genealogist herself.

"I get lost when she starts talking about Ginny's parents, and then all of the Bier priests. I need to see it laid out," she whispered back.

"I know. Lucky for you, I brought along a visual aid." I pointed to the wall in the adjacent family room where I taped up the massive, laminated family tree. Her eyes widened. I decided that, rather than presenting the information-dense document to the group as a whole, I'd hold court near it and whoever was sufficiently interested could question me. I tried to remember that this day wasn't about facts and data, rather about relationships and memories. Kathleen's speech was winding down.

"And then, one day I was on break at work and I got a notice on my phone that I had a new relative on 23andme. I logged on, and you could have knocked me over with a feather when I saw Henry!"

We all turned to look at Henry who stood quietly in a corner during Kathleen's story telling.

"Yes, and you see, that was true for me as well," he said. "I got the information in my initial report, and because Kathleen made so much information about her story public on the site—where she grew up, where she went to school, what she knew about our mother—I knew that it was pretty likely that it was true, that we were brother and sister. But I held off contacting her; she was the first one to reach out." He smiled, motioning the conversation back to Kathleen.

"That pretty much takes us up to now, so I think I'm done, I'll let Henry take it from here." Kathleen glanced at her new brother, silently passing the oratorial baton.

As Henry spoke, I felt like I'd heard him before. Then it struck me—Henry sounded like one of the innumerable priests that I heard during a lifetime of Sundays. He had a measured, calm cadence, with carefully chosen words and sentences that, despite being extemporaneous, seemed prepared. When he paused and folded his hands, resting them lightly on his slightly round belly, I had to stifle a gasp.

I quietly cracked open my laptop and located Father Joseph Bier's obituary photo. I slid it over to my mom, who passed it to Dad. They glanced at me with eyebrows raised and nodded slightly. Henry was a thinner, more fully-haired match for Father Joseph. Although the photo was a copy of a copy, the resemblance was shocking. Before, I favored Father Joe over Father Ed at about 60 / 40. Now I was at 90 / 10.

"This has been a lot to take in," Henry continued. "You have to remember, I just decided to submit my DNA less than three months ago. Like Kathleen, I hired a firm out of Florida to investigate my biological parents. I was raised by actual Fetta parents, who were the most wonderful, kind parents to me and my sister, who was also adopted. I never wanted to do anything that could have possibly hurt them, especially my mother, so I waited until they both passed to begin searching.

"And when the company discovered that all the documents from the Catholic orphanage where I was adopted from were falsified, I was ready to give up. But then my kids gave me the gift of the DNA kit, and I decided why not? I didn't even pause to consider the possibility of something like this," he motioned toward everyone, "let alone a SISTER! I mean, wow, it's just amazing.

"And then to find out everything that Kathleen discovered about our mother, and the work that she and Barb and Angie had been doing to identify our father. I still can't wrap my head around it all. But one thing I am certain of . . ." He cocked his head to the side and motioned with his hand, his lip trembling slightly. "I just have to believe that this is a story about love. After all, love brought all of us together today. All of us, all four of us. That's why I brought the four roses, every person in this story is equally important and loved."

I worried about Henry's assertion that he was sure this was a story rooted in love. What if it wasn't? What if it was a story rooted in abuse, secrecy, scandal? There was the basic problem that their father was a priest, with all the attendant scandalous, shameful baggage. How could a love story possibly be spun of those unholy threads? If their father turned out to be Father Ed, my dad and his cousins would be able to relate all sorts of genuine, heartfelt stories about what a great guy he was. Father Ed could perhaps make the love story salvageable. If the father was Father Joseph, did such a possibility exist? So far, all I had to flesh out his background was a news clipping on a libel lawsuit that ushered in his early retirement.

I refocused as Henry delivered an invocation of good wishes and thanks to God for all present. Barb then did a quick review of the day's itinerary, and I offered to review the family tree if anyone was interested. People wandered over and I helped them make sense of the tree. Kathleen's husband, Mitch, attempted to engage me in a conversation on his interpretation of the relationship data from 23andme. As the forwarded copy of his earlier letter implied, he felt that I was making things too difficult. I decided that this was neither the time nor the place to start a full-on scientific debate.

"Well, I know I'm being a big old wet blanket," I said with forced lightheartedness, "but what can I say? I'm a perfectionist! Luckily, the Nashville conference is in less than a week, and then I'll finally be able to put the genetics question to bed."

"Um-hmm, I'll be interested to see what happens. I know that based on the information that I found online, it looks like Father Ed is the guy."

"We'll see," I said. Awkward.

I continued chit-chatting, highlighting the potential priests in the tree, and noting those that I so far eliminated. I also made a point of highlighting the three brother priests, repeatedly explaining that anyone that we tested in the larger tree would be equally related to all three of them. I reiterated that science alone may not solve this mystery.

At one point, Henry's wife, Lynn, sidled up to me and asked, "So, you're pretty sure it's Father Joseph, aren't you?"

"Yes, but I'm trying to remain open-minded until we can prove things one way or the other, Father Ed or Father Joe," I replied in a low voice.

"Well, you must have some notion of how likely one is over the other, right? You can tell me. I mean, before a month ago, I hadn't ever heard of any of these people, it really makes no difference to me," she said with a smile.

"Oh, I'm 95% percent sure," I blurted, upping my earlier estimate without intending to do so.

"That it's Father Ed," Lynn said hopefully, belying her earlier statement of neutrality.

"No, that it's Father Joe." Yikes, we were miles apart in our understanding, and Lynn's understanding likely reflected Henry's.

We began gathering our belongings to begin a tour of 200 years of Roethle history in Wisconsin. I turned my mental attention from fatherly conjecture to the more settled matter of Kathleen & Henry's mother, Ginny.

* * *

I enlisted Mom as navigator and we drove about ten minutes to our first destination, Old St. John's Cemetery. It was located at the top of a hill, approached through a stand of trees and up a gravel driveway. Barb pointed out where the original Roethle pioneer built his first tiny house in the copse at the bottom of the hill. She claimed that, during the winter when the leaves were down, you could see the base of the original windmill. The cemetery itself used to be attached to a small Catholic chapel that no longer existed. The cemetery was in an idyllic spot, on the top of a glacial moraine, with an expansive view for miles. Clouds scuttled through the sky. On the adjacent property, several industrial windmills churned away, generating power. We identified a number of family tombstones, including a number from the John Roethle family. I was in my element, photographing tombstones and recording dates. I overheard a snippet of conversation in the background that drew my attention.

"Look, a Becker!" Henry exclaimed. "That was the name on our birth certificates, Kathleen. Do you think they're related?"

Kathleen and I walked over to join him. "There were no Beckers anywhere in the family tree," I said. "But if Becker was a name that was common in the area, maybe it was just an easy place-filler for Ginny? Are there any Rohners?" I asked, recalling the other sham last name. We searched around but didn't find any.

Henry and Kathleen posed for a few photos in front of tombstones, but I could tell by their questions and expressions that their hearts weren't fully in it. I could understand why. The cemetery was the territory of Barb, my mother, and me—genealogy nerds interested in cobbling together facts of the distant past. It had little to do with their mother's life story.

We climbed back in our cars to make the quick drive to our next stop: The John and Katherine Roethle farm, Ginny's grandparents, Henry and Kathleen's great-grandparents, and my great-great grandparents.

As we walked to our cars, Kathleen rushed over, texting furiously. "I heard from Ted earlier, saying that he might be able to bring Jerome. Now they're about 30 minutes away. I'm going to arrange to have them meet us at the next house." She was practically quivering with excitement. To me, the whole day was filled with new people and new introductions, so the significance of this really didn't hit me at first. But Kathleen's inquisitive mind never rested. Had she managed to convince the mysteriously reticent Ted to bring his father, Jerome, to talk with Kathleen and Henry? Jerome would be meeting his niece and nephew for the first time. Did he know that his sister, Ginny, left behind children when she died? Did he suspect?

I barely had time to turn over these questions as Barb led our caravan into the next driveway down the road. We approached the

John Roethle farm. This was the childhood home of Leo, Rosalie, Oscar, and their unmarried siblings—the people in the studio portrait. Barb warned us that she had talked with the fellow who owned the John Roethle farm. He agreed to let us in but cautioned that the place wasn't much to look at. No one lived there for some time and he rented out the surrounding fields rather than farming them himself. Barb asked for a five-minute head start to meet with the property owner and get the situation squared away.

We pulled into a rutted gravel driveway. The house appeared forgotten, left to return to nature. It had the overgrown, weed-studded lawn of abandonment. Mom and I joined the line of cars parked in front of several weather-worn barns and outbuildings that collapsed onto themselves, finally surrendering to time and neglect. Across the weedy yard, Barb conferred with a man who quickly disappeared. She motioned us over.

"He says we should go in here, but be careful because the electricity doesn't work and in some places the floor is caving in," said Barb, pointing to a door. "He owns the place, but no one is living here. This would have been where John and Katherine raised their family. I remember hearing about the grand red and white house when I was a kid, and I have some pictures. But no one has lived here for years..." She motioned to the tired, gray building.

Some old farmhouses give the impression that they could fade away and disappear with an errant breeze. They tend to be small, unremarkable, and cheaply built. They project impermanence. Despite being abandoned, though, this house seemed much more rooted to the place. It was broad and low, with rows of intact windows. It was neglected, but it was solid and didn't plan to give up any time soon.

I tried to imagine a family of eight children working and playing here. It seemed impossible. The house was simply too dark, too foreboding, too hollow. Whether the place was whispering stories to me or not, it was still an old treasure that needed exploring. I pulled out my phone and turned on the flashlight. The door we entered was a cellar type door, down two broad stone steps, leading to a ramshackle mud room. As we crossed the next threshold, we entered what once was a formal parlor. There were outward-facing windows on the opposite side of the room as well. It wasn't a cellar, but a semi-exposed lower level.

I peered through my beam of light, motes gently swirling through the room. I imagined people moving through this room, gathered for family holidays or prayers. Here in the dark, ghost-hunter atmosphere, the place seemed imminently more evocative than it had from the outside. I carefully walked across the floor, avoiding places where the wide, weathered boards splintered. I admired beautiful old wainscoting, thick trim work and window casings ornate with deep, gracious sills. Bits of faded blue wallpaper clung on for dear life. At one time, this room had been the centerpiece of a grand farmhouse. I walked to the opposite wall and peered across the threshold into the next room and saw with alarm that the floor was almost entirely caved in. Barb made nervous noises behind me, and I took the hint. I suddenly noticed that the air was uncomfortably stuffy and musty, and decided that I had enough of the beautiful, ghostly, toxic room. Light leaked in from a stairwell, and several other members of our group journeyed up. I followed them. Incandescent light spilled down the stairs, but hadn't Barb said that the electricity was turned off?

The second level must have been where more recent occupants of the house stayed. It showed some attempts at refurbishing. There was a linoleum kitchen and a carpeted family room lined with sagging furniture. Not-at-all-dusty empty beer bottles rested on windowsills, and a bed in a back room was made with rumpled sheets. Someone either lived or squatted here, a far spookier prospect than the ghostly dimness of the lower level. I snapped a quick picture of a photo of the farm on the wall. It was one of those taken by a low-flying plane, probably sometime in the 1980s, when the exterior remained neat and cared for.

I exited from the opposite corner of the house than we entered. Once again at ground level, I gulped the fresh air. Mom and I agreed that there were weird vibes on that upper level and decided to focus our exploratory efforts on the outbuildings.

Just outside the door stood a small stone building with a chimney and an entrance threshold smoothed concave. I suspect that it once was a summer kitchen; a peek inside revealed a broad fireplace perfect for cooking. Barb pointed out a machine shed across the yard and encouraged us to explore.

I pulled open the weather-worn door and stepped inside. There was an old burn barrel full of empty beer cans. Next to it stood a milk jug with the name "Edwin Roethle" painted on it. Cool. As my eyes adjusted to the light, I saw black stenciling on the barn boards adjacent to the doorway. "Ignatz Roethle" and "John Roethle" were inscribed in succession. They autographed the barn! I greedily snapped photos on my phone. This was the type of nerdy evidence that sent my heart racing. Other than stale old hay and a few more scattered beer cans, the space was empty. I stepped outside, planning to grab my parents to see the names on the wall. While I was geeking out in the granary, a gray minivan pulled up. My dad leaned against the passenger side door, talking to the shriveled man inside.

Mom, walked quickly over to me, her eyebrows raised in excitement.

"Is Jerome here?" I asked.

"Yes, and you'll never believe what he said," she said. "So, Dad starts talking to him, you know the way he does, chatting about this and that. 'Do you remember so-and-so?' and 'did you ever visit such-and-such a place?' And then, real casually, he asks, 'Say, did your sister Ginny ever keep house for a priest?' And Jerome answers without missing a beat, 'Yeah, she kept house for Father Joe Bier.'" Mom looked at me, waiting for my response.

I was gobsmacked! "So, I guess that's about as clear as it's going to get, huh?" I said. "Did Henry or Kathleen hear him?"

"No," said Mom, "but then the old guy's son came over to get him out of the car, and your dad went over and told Henry and Kathleen."

"Wow. Just wow," I said. I walked over to Dad to confirm the story, and he repeated back the same conversation verbatim. Jerome sat in a wheelchair, and a man who must be his son stood at his shoulder.

Kathleen, in full investigation mode, squatted next to him, leaning on the arm of the wheelchair, gently drawing Jerome into conversation. Molly stood in the background, recording the conversation. Clearly, everyone realized the significance of the information that Jerome had to share. I looked around for Henry. He lingered back from the group.

"How are you doing?" I asked, putting a hand on his arm.

"Well, I'm just surprised. It looks like it must be Father Joseph? I didn't expect that. . ." Henry trailed off as he turned inward to deal with this new bit of information. He was visibly shaken.

I left Henry with his thoughts and returned to the group gathered around Jerome. He was a gaunt old man, with loose fitting dentures. He was fond of a joke, and every time he laughed, I worried for the safety of those rattling dentures. His dementia was such that Jerome recalled events of the far past with remarkable clarity, but had little handle on the present. For example, his daughter-in-law came along on the trip. She was Ted's wife, and they lived near his nursing home and visited frequently. Despite this, Jerome greeted her several times as a "another long-lost cousin, nice to meet you."

I supposed that his recollections would have to be taken with a grain of salt. But the report of Ginny "keeping house for Father Joe Bier" was huge. All these months we wondered where Ginny was sent after dropping out of the convent. We finally had an answer. Was the genetic confirmation even necessary at this point? I suspected that Kathleen "The Spit Is It" LeFranc would still want them.

Kathleen gently introduced the notion that she was Ginny's daughter, that Henry over there was Ginny's son. Jerome nodded politely, the nod of false comprehension, fooling no one. It seemed that Jerome had no idea that Ginny ever had a child. Earlier, Liz said that Ginny's pregnancy was known by the family. Jerome's reactions suggested that only *some* of the family knew—most likely the women.

Jerome spoke of his and Ginny's mother, and how difficult it was for her to be widowed at such a young age. He kept repeating, "She did the best she could." Helen (Bier) Roethle was widowed at 49. At the time, the children ranged in age from Eugene at 24 to David at 10. Ginny was

15, Jerome 12. It seems that Helen's best included attempting to place the kids out of the home where possible. Jerome remembered that Ginny took their father's death "pretty hard," and implied that she and Helen butted heads. But he never directly chastised his mother's treatment of Ginny, carefully always going back to the assertion that she did her best. It must have been so hard.

Jerome didn't see Ginny much after she left for the convent, and then to keep house for Father Joe. He didn't know how long she was with him, or if she ever kept house for anyone else. He did recall that she started drinking "pretty regular" as she got older, and that she had a generally disappointing, sad life. Liz suggested that her Aunt Ginny might have let slip some of the details of her pregnancies during these later drinking years.

Jerome maintained not a glimmer of recognition to the storyline of "Ginny as mother." He remained as blankly bemused at the end of the 15-minute conversation as he was at the beginning. Kathleen and Henry, who eventually joined the circle, were just a couple more long-lost cousins. Nothing more, nothing less. His dementia-attacked mind did not include a blank space for "Ginny's kids."

Jerome quickly grew tired. Kathleen and Henry thanked Ted profusely for bringing his father along, and he loaded Jerome back into the van, anxious to return him to the comforting routine of the memory care unit. Jerome flashed us a last, loose-dentured grin before being hoisted into the passenger seat. As for the rest of us? The last stop of the morning would be at Jerome and Ginny's childhood home in Neosho, the home where Leo and Helen raised their kids. The home that received Ginny from the failed life at the convent and sent her on to keep house for Father Joseph Bier.

Casebook summary

• A much clearer picture of Ginny's life as a child and young woman is emerging

•Jerome's statement placing Ginny with Father Joseph Bier is the best piece of evidence that we've gotten so far.

    oFind confirmatory genetic evidence to support his recollections

Potential Fathers

Edward Bier (highly unlikely)
~~Robert Gassert~~
Robert Bier (highly unlikely)
**Joseph Bier
Francis Bier (highly unlikely)
~~Charles Bier~~
~~Raymond Parr~~

The John Roethle family. Leo Roethle, Ginny's father, is in the front row on the left. Oscar Roethle, Barb's grandfather, is in the front row on the right. Rosalie (Roethle) Bier, my great-grandmother, is in the back row on the right.

Henry and Kathleen's first meeting

Fr. Joseph Bier, age 42

Henry Fetta, age 60

A comparison of Henry and Father Joseph.

The ghostly interior of the John Roethle home.

Jerome Roethle talking with Kathleen and Henry.

Chapter Sixteen
Duck Inn, Duck Out

The rest of the day felt...surface-ish. The John and Katherine Roethle home oozed with history, both inside and out. From the ghostly and creepy interior to the encounter with Jerome outside, the place was imbued with significance and meaning. After that, every stop paled in comparison. In retrospect, we tried to cram too much stuff in to a single day. Too many places, too many meetings.

We left the home of their great-grandparents and drove about ten minutes or so to Ginny's childhood home. Kathleen and Henry's biological grandfather, Leo Roethle, married Helen Bier in 1922; this was the second Roethle-Bier marriage. The first was between my own great-grandparents. Leo and Helen took up farming in the next village over. Of all of John and Katherine's children, the only one to make a significant move away from the stately farmhouse was Rosalie, my great-grandmother, when she moved all the way to the Valentine Bier farm.

On the drive to Helen and Leo Roethle's former home, Mom and I turned over the significance of Jerome's revelations. Did Ginny ever come back to visit her family? Did Father Joe ever come with her? Did her mother, Helen, know about the pregnancies? Did she suspect??

"I do need to thank you, Mom," I said as I drove.

"For what? Teaching you how to do tombstone rubbings?" She laughed.

"No. For never forcing me to go to the convent—or anywhere else, for that matter." I couldn't get past the notion that somehow, Ginny was trying to escape these idyllic rolling hills and her family when she began living with Father Joseph.

"I always said that I didn't care if you kids became president or a hairdresser," she replied in a familiar refrain, "just as long as you were happy."

We drove into the village of Neosho and pulled onto a road running parallel to the main drag. We quickly located the former Leo and Helen Roethle house. It backed up to a nameless creek which drained the Neosho Millpond and sat across the street from a baseball field. The property bore some vestiges of the working farm that it once was—a few outbuildings and the old-fashioned shrubs and perennials of the Wisconsin countryside. For the most part, though, it was an unremarkable, modernized bungalow. The owner, a no-nonsense woman in her 50s, met us outside and chatted with Kathleen and Barb about the improvements she made to the place, her gardens, and other standard topics of rural conversation. There was nothing ghostly, evocative, or sentimental about either her or the light-blue-sided home.

My notes indicated that Leo was a farmer by profession before dying at the age of 50. Helen taught school in the Janesville area until her marriage brought her to the Roethle lands. There she remained, outliving Leo by 50 years and eventually dying at age 103. Helen had eight children, but only four grandchildren—that she knew of. That number now grew to six, including Kathleen and Henry. Liz, her sister, and Jerome's two boys were the only grandchildren that ever marauded the bluffs and creek beds on which we now stood.

I broke away from the group and wandered into the backyard. It was the only bit of the property that was still somewhat vintage. Old-fashioned bridal's wreath, peonies, lilac bushes dotted the lawn. I wandered toward the bluff at the edge of the backyard and tried to get a feel for the place. How did Helen and Leo raise their children? There were reports of now-elderly neighbors who remembered sledding with the Roethle kids down the bluffs to a winter-frozen creek. So, there must have been *some* room for fun.

But all could not have been well in the family. Liz's father was the oldest child, and Liz no longer had anything to do with him. There was Jerome, and then there were two more brothers who didn't keep in touch with the family at all. One of them lived "out west, Idaho or somewhere," according to Liz. And finally, the youngest son died at 27. Among the three girls, all of them spent time in the convent. We knew how that turned out for Ginny. One became a teaching nun for a time, and eventually left religious life and married a former monk. The third sister joined a missionary order in Asia before returning home to care for the aging Helen.

So, there weren't a lot of family reunions after Leo and Helen Roethle's kids left home. Without more first-hand accounts to fill in the story, I instead identified a pattern of escaping. Escaping what? Perhaps the children longed to leave rural life, or intense religiosity, or the cold climate, or a house overshadowed by the early death of a beloved father. Or maybe it was just the way it happened, an unintentional drifting apart.

I turned to walk back from the bluff. Across the lawn, Henry stood alone next to a bed of Oriental lilies, his hands clasped behind his back, gazing into the middle distance. I imagined that he, too, looked for a sign of his mother's presence. I felt his disappointment but realized that there was nothing more that I could offer to bring this place alive. It was just a house. The stories attached to it no longer lived there.

When we drove into town, I noticed On the Rocks Bar and Grill on the main drag. By now, my stomach was rumbling and my brain was full. I couldn't be the only one feeling this way. I suggested to Barb that we might want to grab a bite. She agreed, but there was one other person that she wanted Henry and Kathleen to meet, a local who palled around with the Roethle kids. I offered to lead the rest of the group to the restaurant and get started ordering some food for everyone while Kathleen and Henry had their meeting.

On the Rocks was just what the doctor ordered. The cozy, wood-paneled bar and grill quickly fueled us with pizzas, Spotted Cow beer, and normalcy. Eventually, Barb, Kathleen, and Henry rejoined us. We talked over the amazing morning and the interesting people we met. There tended to be several conversations always going on simultaneously, as our group spanned several tables pushed together.

At one point, I turned to Kathleen and asked about the elderly citizen that she and Henry met.

"Oh, he remembered the Roethles and sledding with them on the hill," she replied. "When I told him about me and Henry, he seemed surprised, but only because he heard that Ginny had an abortion," she continued, eyebrows raised.

"Wow," I said, "So I guess there was some idea of what was going on then, huh?"

"Seems like it."

"So then, how in the world did Jerome not know about it? How open was this pregnancy?" I wondered.

"I know," said Kathleen. "The whole thing is just unbelievable. And who know if there weren't more pregnancies or abortions that actually happened?"

I nodded silently. What more could we say? We turned to rejoin the group's chatter. Chatter about Wisconsin, Illinois, families, grandkids, and stories of growing up. While we were far-flung relatives, we quickly formed a camaraderie and understanding that made conversation easy.

Through all the chatter, I began to have a nagging worry in the pit of my stomach. If Father Joseph was, in fact, their father, then I wasn't really all that closely related to them at all. I didn't have a great grasp on the story of that branch of the Bier family tree, that of Frank Bier and his three priest sons. Would a trip to Janesville just to visit the pioneer farmhouse of Father Joseph's grandfather really be worth the hour plus drive? Contrary to my worries, everyone insisted that, "Yes, yes," they wanted to go.

"And," Kathleen reminded me, "remember that a couple of the Parr kids in Janesville were going to meet us, so they'll be expecting us."

So, it was settled. I tried to get the group moving quickly to squeeze in the tail end of the itinerary. When I mentioned this, Barb said, "Yes, we only have one more stop to make here—we have to go to Ginny's grave."

"Is it with the rest of the family the cemetery down the road?" I asked, nervous for time.

"No, Ginny is actually buried about 15 miles south of here, next to the man who she was with later in life. They never got married, no one really liked him, and it wasn't a particularly happy relationship, but that's what she chose," Barb said.

So, Ginny was left to piece her life together after Father Joe moved on to his final parish and, eventually, retirement. Poor Ginny. Poor, poor Ginny.

* * *

I made the executive decision that, for this bit at least, Kathleen and Henry and their spouses should have this moment alone with their mother's grave. I suggested that the rest of us begin the drive over to Janesville and the Valentine Bier farm. The plan was adopted, GPSs programmed, and off we went.

As we crossed into Rock County, about 60 miles south of the Roethle homes, the landscape changed dramatically. The extreme southern part of Wisconsin, where the Biers farmed, is a wide swath of fertile flat farmland that stretches for miles to the horizon. Instead of the dramatic hills of Neosho and Rubicon, I grew up surrounded by rich agricultural land with black, loamy soil over a foot deep. My mom was fond of repeating something she read about this being "the best farmland in the world, along with some place in Russia." This was usually followed by a tsk-tsking admonition about whatever development was being proposed at the time.

The summer sun was just beginning to dip into the western sky, lending that glorious pinkish glow to the corn and soybean fields. This was the backdrop of my childhood. We drove down the familiar country roads that intersected predictably at every mile, in the orderly plat lines laid out hundreds of years ago. We ended up at the Valentine Bier farmhouse, what was now referred to as "Auntie Eleanor's place." The farm passed from Valentine to his youngest son, Edward. Edward married Rosalie Roethle and raised their Four Bier Boys there, including Father Ed Bier and my Grandpa Vince. The youngest of the

Four Bier Boys was Alfie. He and his wife Eleanor raised ten kids of their own at the place. Now, the only person left from the Four Bier Boys' generation was Auntie Eleanor. The majority of the farming operation was sold off when the Biers were forced out of farming during the agricultural downturn of the 1980s. Nonetheless, the farmhouse remained a touchstone for many of the Biers that still lived on the Rock Prairie. Auntie Eleanor maintained an open-door policy, and several of her children stopped in daily. She hosted cards once a week on Tuesday night. Mom and Dad stopped by with blessed communion bread and wine every Sunday after mass. It was familiar territory.

We parked at the end of the driveway, in front of the pig barn that was converted to "Bob's Man Cave." Bob was one of Alfie and Eleanor's sons, and it was common knowledge that when he inherited the property, he planned to raze the tired old farmhouse. The original barn was already long gone.

As thoughts of architectural salvage danced through my head, I forced my focus on the mystery at hand. Eleanor *must* have met both Ginny and Father Joseph. Eleanor's husband, Alfie, and Ginny were first cousins; they shared a Grandma and Grandpa John Roethle. Uncle Alfie was also Father Joseph's cousin; they shared a Grandma and Grandpa Valentine Bier. I hoped that we'd be able to gain some insights from her.

I met Dad's cousin, Joan, outside my car. Joan was another one of Eleanor's ten children. I had left it to her to prepare Eleanor for our arrival, to attempt to explain the situation in advance, and to manage the business of not overwhelming her. Eleanor was a tough old broad, but she was also 86. Joan gave the back door a cursory knock—I'm not sure that the front door was even functional—and ushered us through the mud room and into the small kitchen.

"Mother," Joan yelled as we entered, "I've got Tom and Janice and Angie here!"

"Hello," Eleanor said, looking up from her euchre hand. Not surprisingly, she was playing cards in the adjacent dining room. Euchre is a traditional German card game and is frequently used as a warm-up to the more advanced game favored by the Biers, Five Hundred. Several of Eleanor's grandchildren played with her.

"Well, Mother, it's been an interesting day. We went over to the old Roethle place," said Joan.

"Oh yes," Eleanor replied, still studying her cards through her bifocals, "what was that like?"

"It was illuminating," I said. "Do you remember Ginny Roethle?"

"Yes..."

"I'm not sure if Joan told you, but come to find out she had two kids that she gave up for adoption," I said.

"I remember you saying something about that," she replied, glancing at my father. That's right—months ago, Dad asked her whether Father Ed might have had children, back when he was still the main contender. I was relieved that she had some familiarity with the story, at least.

"And I know Dad asked you if Father Ed could have been the father, and I know you don't think so, and neither do I. We're pretty sure it was Father Joe Bier," I continued. No point in confusing her with all of the muddled eventualities and backstories.

"Father Joe?" Confusion creased her forehead, and she set her cards down. Her granddaughters were mildly annoyed to have their game interrupted, but at this point, I had to go all in. I opened up a can of worms, and now I needed to deal with them.

"I know it sounds crazy, but Father Joe Bier, Frank and Mary Bier's son, one of the three priest brothers. We figured it out through the DNA, and then today, we met Jerome Roethle, Ginny's brother, and he told us that Ginny was Father Joe's housekeeper. So that pretty much seals the deal."

Eleanor raised her hands slightly, along with her eyebrows and pursed her lips. Oh dear, we were overwhelming her. I don't think that Joan could have fully prepared her for all this.

During this exchange, one of the granddaughters listened intently. While Eleanor was a bit confused, she got it.

"So, wait," she said, "they were living together in the rectory and had not one, but TWO kids? This sounds just like *The Thornbirds*...And you're sure it's not Father Ed?"

"I know, it's unbelievable, and, yes, I'm pretty sure that it wasn't Father Ed." She looked relieved. "And these two kids, Henry and Kathleen, just met each other for the first time today. They're headed this way cuz they want to see where the Biers are from, and whether your grandma might remember anything about the people involved." I finished. It was the simplest I could make it. Whew.

I turned to Eleanor, at this point completely derailing the card game, and started in on my questions. Eleanor's answers were perfunctory at best. She knew of the people involved, but not particularly well. Just sketches of each of them.

Did she ever meet Ginny? "I suppose I met her once or twice..."

Did she remember Father Joe? "Yes, Father Joe...he was FAT."

What about the other brothers? "Well, Father Fran.... he was OLD. And Father Bob, he was..." shrug with a slightly bemused grimace.

What about Frank and Mary Bier, the parents of the three priest brothers? What was their family like? "Now, Mary Bier, she wanted all those kids in the convent or the seminary, THAT I remember. And Agnes, the daughter, she went a little cuckoo."

And finally, "Jerome Roethle? Yes, I remember him. One time when the kids were still little and Alfie was gone, he showed up here, looking for a place to stay." Eleanor made each of these pronouncements with her usual no-nonsense practicality.

And just as quickly as Eleanor engaged with the line of inquiry, she seemed to pull away. Unfortunately, the party was just beginning. While this conversation was going on, a handful more cars pulled up, carrying some of the Janesville Parr relatives, known to me only as names from 23andme. I went to greet them and quickly realized it would be impossible and unwise to make introductions, let alone fit more people in the dining room. So, Mom and Dad kept them busy in the kitchen, looking at photo albums and family trees, while Joan managed things with her mom in the dining room. I glanced out the kitchen window and saw Henry's and Kathleen's cars pull up.

I was mortified that they drove all this way for what would amount to not much. If Father Ed were still a serious contender, this was at least his birth home. Since our focus shifted in the past five hours, the connection to the place was much more tenuous. And I didn't want to push things with Auntie Eleanor. I took a deep, overwhelmed breath and exited the mud room into the dusky light.

"Hello, how was your drive?" I asked.

"Fine, fine," Henry said.

"And did you find Ginny's grave?"

"Yes, Kathleen and I were able to spend some time there. It was very special."

"So, I've been to Janesville before with Barb, but never out here," Kathleen said.

"Yes, "I replied, "this is the Rock Prairie, and this is the home that Valentine Bier built. The original barn is gone, and the pig barn is a rec room now, so there is not necessarily a ton of historical things to look at, but I thought you'd want to see the place itself. Get a feel for the area. Father Joseph's dad, Frank, was raised here, and he planted that row of cottonwood trees lining the driveway," I said.

Henry smiled, clasping his hands behind his back and staring off across the cottonwood trees to the spreading prairie.

"Are the Parrs here yet? I'm looking forward to seeing them," Kathleen said, again reminding me of how extensive her connections and work were by this stage of the game.

"Yes, they're here, along with Eleanor and a handful of her grandkids. So, remember, Eleanor is Father Ed's sister-in-law. Cousin by marriage to Father Joseph and Ginny. I wasn't sure how much she'd know of them, but she remembered a few things. I'm afraid, though, that we might have overwhelmed her. I'm not sure how much conversation she has left...."

"Oh, I want to go in and pay my respects either way," said Henry.

"Yes, definitely," Kathleen said.

So, I took them in, through the crowded kitchen, and into the crowded dining room where Eleanor continued to hold increasingly confused court. The conversation had shifted to *The Thornbirds.* I interrupted and introduced Henry and Kathleen, and Eleanor greeted them with a perfectly polite, "Pleased to meetcha." And then I left the two siblings to it.

I stayed in the kitchen, trying to keep the Parrs entertained and not overrunning the dining room. Kathleen attempted to make a connection with Eleanor in the same way that she had with Jerome, squatting next to her chair, and repeating that she was Ginny's daughter. Eleanor never really got it, I don't think. She never really grasped who Henry and Kathleen were to her, because she never was all that close to either Ginny or Father Joseph. I think that she felt understandably overwhelmed and decided not to spend any more mental energy trying to sort the whole thing out. To this day, I feel badly that we didn't manage that visit better. I wanted to show Henry and Kathleen a representation of the Bier-ness of being a Bier, but the visit was too rushed, too confusing, too overcrowded.

We ended up staying for only about ten minutes more, during which time Father Ed's name was re-introduced, which confused Eleanor even further. I kept repeating, "But we don't think it's him," to little effect. Joan finally took over and started shifting the group towards the door. Out of respect for Eleanor's already-invaded privacy, and our long-since-passed dinner reservation, we said goodbye and formed a caravan of cars on the prairie roads to make the drive to dinner.

I found out later that Eleanor was, in fact, quite flustered by the visit. The questions and the number of people were just overwhelming. I took my father's word for it that he smoothed everything over in his typical "let's just all get along" fashion. I tried to forgive myself for mismanaging the visit. But latent Catholicism is hard to shake, and I still feel guilty when reflecting on that evening. By that point, I needed a drink.

* * *

We drove to The Duck Inn, my favorite supper club, a few miles east of the Bier farms. Located smack in the middle of nowhere, this was a supper club in the classic sense of the phrase. As near as I can tell, supper clubs are very much a regional phenomenon, and have something to do with granting liquor licenses only to places that also served meals, or supper. Supper clubs dot the state of Wisconsin, and the most authentic—and best, in my opinion—are rural. Their decor is simple, the cuts of meat generous, and the brandy old fashioneds strong. Supper club fare should include a bread basket featuring individually wrapped crackers, a relish tray, and end up with a generous selection of ice cream drinks. The Duck Inn had these in spades, plus they could accommodate a group of 25.

By the time my parents and I arrived, the rest of the group was seated, and we squeezed into the end of the table. A spirit of easy familiarity settled over our motley crew, probably aided by the prompt bar service. Multiple conversations were in full swing up and down the table. Kathleen sat in the middle, and glowed with happiness as she chatted with all of the friends and relations that she gathered together over the past several years of searching. I sat next to Henry, who was quieter, but exuded contentment. True to form, as soon as our drinks arrived delivered, he rose to give a toast.

I'd be lying if I said that I remember his exact words, and I won't try to recreate them. He stood next to Kathleen, and, with a hand on her shoulder, invoked love, family, surprises and the hand of God working through the people gathered. He toasted Barb and me, and I suppose that I laughed and said something self-effacing. I have detailed memories and notes on so many aspects of this story, but not of this dinner. Instead of details, I recall a general sense of satisfaction.

As I polished off my duck, I realized that I didn't know how long it would be before I saw Henry or Kathleen again. Their families were getting together the next day, but I would return to Milwaukee. So, it was time to get in any questions that needed asking. I set down my fork.

"How are you feeling about everything, Henry? About the fact that it's looking more like Father Joe is the one, I mean?"

"I have to admit that I'm feeling a little disappointed. The only things we seem to know about him are that he was something of a scoundrel."

I nodded sympathetically and returned to my plate. What could I say to that? I didn't know much more about him, but maybe there was more to the story. I began plotting my next move.

We wrapped up dinner with hugs and promises to keep in touch. Henry and Lynn would host Kathleen and her husband the next day for a backyard barbeque. All his kids would be there to meet their new aunt. I secured promises that pictures would be taken. As I pulled out into the dark prairie road to make the drive back to Milwaukee, my mind was already on to the next step: Nashville to confirm our suspicions through modern genetics, and then investigating the person that was Father Joseph Bier. How much of a scoundrel was he, really?

Casebook summary

- •Confirm or deny Father Joseph as most likely
- oGenetics conference in Nashville this weekend
- •Research Father Joseph & Ginny at St. Francis Xavier church

Potential Fathers

Edward Bier (highly unlikely)

~~Robert Gassert~~

Robert Bier (highly unlikely)

**Joseph Bier

Francis Bier (highly unlikely)

~~Charles Bier~~

~~Raymond Parr~~

Ginny's grave, St. Joan of Arc Cemetery, Oconomowoc, Wisconsin

The Valentine Bier home, at which Eleanor Bier still resides.

Backyard get-together at the Fetta home. From L-R, Martin (Kathleen's husband), Kathy Brummel (the daughter who remembered Ginny from when her family hosted her during her pregnancy), Kathleen, Henry, Lynn (Henry's wife), and their children & grandchildren.

Chapter Seventeen
Nashville

How have I never been to Nashville before? I mused, riding in an Uber on the way to meet Louise. The bones of the central historic city were surrounded by sprawling suburbs, and the entire metro area was dotted with tempting restaurants. Our hotel was just off Music Row, the site of famous recording studios. It was also just a couple of blocks away from the campus of Vanderbilt University. The lobby was charming and modern, with large art installations and the unique decor that endeared Kimpton hotels to both Louise and me. My sister arrived several hours before I did. When I unlocked our room, I found her just emerging from a nap, rooftop swim, and shower. We laughed and hugged and sprawled on our beds. I caught her up on the events of the Roethle reunion, and she caught me up on her life in New York. It was good to see her.

We arrived on a Friday and left on Sunday. We decided to focus on genetics Saturday afternoon and spend the rest of the time relaxing. Since neither of us really cared one way or another about music, we took in the culinary scene. We enjoyed a walk on the gorgeous, tree-studded Vanderbilt campus. We swung side by side in ingenious slatted swings in Memorial Park; they were somehow propelled by flexing and extending your ankles. There were cocktails, there was binge-watching of *The Unbreakable Kimmy Schmidt.* It was lovely.

And on Saturday, we got down to work. Louise plopped onto her bed and logged into a program called PopLink. This is a program designed by the Lincoln Park Zoo "to be used in the analysis and management of studbook databases." A studbook is not, as it sounds, a forerunner of Tinder, but rather a system used in the management of breeding animals in zoos. Any zoo worth its salt is a member of the Association of Zoos and Aquariums, headquartered at the Lincoln Park

Zoo in Chicago. And such a membership requires, for many species, that a studbook be maintained.

> The purpose of a . . .studbook is to document the pedigree and entire demographic history of each animal within a managed population. . . These collective histories, compiled and maintained by an Association of Zoos and Aquariums Regional Studbook Keeper, are known as the population's genetic and demographic identity and are valuable tools to track and manage each individual as part of a single *ex situ* population. (9)

As Kathleen and Henry's insane luck would have it, Louise had been a Regional Studbook Keeper at the Lincoln Park Zoo. For several years, she assisted species management groups with breeding plans to maintain a genetically healthy population. From orangutans to migratory birds, she was there, virtual studbook in hand, charting the tangled family trees of zoo populations.

What do this weird job and PopLink have to do with Kathleen and Henry? The Bier-Roethle-Parr family trees were not straightforward and simple. Instead, those years-ago Bohemians intermarried for generations, both in the old country and for a few generations more when they arrived in Wisconsin. When presenting results, 23andme assumed simplicity. Kathleen and Henry's relationship to any other Ketzelsdorf descendants could not be easily analyzed by the facile assumptions of 23andme. Instead, we needed a program that could account for tangled. We needed PopLink. And through the miracle of modern electronics, it was there for us in a Nashville hotel room.

While she booted up the computer, I unrolled my six-foot long, laminated family tree. I taped it to the wardrobe, and numbered all the individuals that needed charting in PopLink. We identified 52 key people, going back to Adalbert Bier, the common ancestor from the 19th century that linked the Parrs and Biers. He was born in 1827. The youngest was yours truly, born in 1975. Of course, Henry and Kathleen were included, as were the other modern relatives that showed up in

23andme. These included Liz Mueller, Barb Surwillo, and Dennis Parr. We all became numbers in PopLink.

The program asked for pedestrian data on each of the numbered individuals, such as gender, year of birth, parents if known. It also asked for data that were obviously zoological in nature: Is the participant contracepted / not contracepted / neuter sterile? Is the dam or sire wild? Is the participant live-bearing or egg-laying? We laughed as we answered these, and assumed that everyone was wild, not contracepted, and not egg-laying.

The bulk of the work was data entry and a fastidious attention to detail. These data were then filtered through another program that spit out a number: the predicted percentage of shared DNA between any two numbered individuals in the program. This number happened to be *the same value measured in 23andme's ancestry report!* Finally, we had a way to definitively interpret 23andme's results in light of the complex Bier/Roethle/Parr tree!

Which potential priest father best explained the relationship results that we saw on 23andme? To answer this, Louise and I ran different scenarios through the PopLink program. In each scenario, we made a different priest Kathleen's and Henry's father, including those I already tentatively eliminated from the list. We also ran scenarios for a hypothetical, non-related male. We aimed for scholarly thoroughness and complete datasets in our gorgeous Excel spreadsheets. Finally, for each scenario, we compared PopLink's predicted degrees of relatedness with the measured degrees of relatedness from 23andme. I summarized the results in a letter to Kathleen and Henry:

From: Me
To: Kathleen LeFranc, Henry Fetta
CC: Louise Bier

Dear Kathleen & Henry,
First of all, thanks so much for providing the reason for Louise and I to have a much-needed getaway together. We stayed at a great hotel in Nashville, have had some nice meals and some nice walks on the

Vanderbilt campus which was just a couple of blocks away. It's a gorgeous campus with towering old trees of multiple varieties. Our work on the genealogy mystery took only, really, about three hours of sustained focus. However, we both agree that our everyday lives would have never supported this degree of focus. Further, we both needed to be in the same room to make it happen. So, our research trip was absolutely necessary! :)

[Here I explained our process, described above.]

Anyway, first, we confirmed that your birth father does lie somewhere in the Valentine Bier family tree. When we posited a non-related father and ran the numbers, the numbers were way off, as we assumed. Then we ran test scenarios for all of the potential priests.

If Father Ed was your father, I should be <u>much</u> more related to both of you than I actually am on 23andme. Same for the other eliminated priests. There were only two scenarios that worked.

Genetically speaking, the most likely priest fathers are: Father Joseph Bier OR one of his brothers, OR Father Robert Gassert. We already know that historical data makes Father Robert Gassert an impossibility, given that he was in Kansas and Rome during the critical time period of 1950-1955. In contrast, all three priest brothers were somewhere in the Archdiocese of Milwaukee. Now, we'll never be able to <u>genetically</u> differentiate between Father Joe and either of his two brothers. We have to rely on historical data, i.e., who was where, when.

So, where does that leave us? With the suspicions that we had after the Roethle Reunion confirmed—that Father Joseph Bier is your biological father.

Next steps? Louise and I came up with good test subjects from each of the family clans to definitively confirm or deny Father Ed v. Father Joe (or his brothers). My dad is the test subject from the Father Ed scenario and has already sent off his sample. The test subject for Father Joe is his nephew, Hugh Raddenbach, who I've had several correspondences with. He lives in Alma, Wisconsin, northwest of Madison. Depending on both of your opinions, I would recommend contacting Hugh Raddenbach and seeing if he'd be willing to be tested. Hugh might also be an interesting person to start talking to in terms of what that family was like—if you are interested.

Finally, I personally would be interested in visiting St. Francis Xavier where she worked for him, and seeing if the priest there might be interested in helping us check employment records, etc. Interestingly, he was a former Episcopal priest and made the switch to the Roman Catholic Church—bringing his wife along with him. I await both of your further direction!

xoxo

AB

The results were a bit anticlimactic, but absolutely necessary. We already strongly suspected Father Joseph, the numbers were purely confirmatory. However, from the beginning of our correspondence, Kathleen's mantra was, "The spit is it." Therefore, without definitive genetic proof, none of us could call the case closed. And while I mentally eliminated Father Ed several weeks ago, I knew that we needed to confirm the case with my father's DNA. If he, Henry and Kathleen weren't related at least as much as first cousins, it wasn't Father Ed. We'd have to wait and see. Of course, after meeting Kathleen and Henry, it became suddenly quite easy to convince Dad to spit. He was taken with both of them and remains an avid fan of Henry.

While I waited to hear back from them, Louise and I enjoyed a leisurely afternoon in the rooftop pool, sipping drinks and avoiding other people's attempts at conversation. We had to catch up on important sisterly things, like the state of everyone else in the family, our own lives, and the amazing fact that we were both over 40 years old. We agreed, under that warm Tennessee summer sun, that we felt like we might as well still be wandering around the farm on the Rock Prairie.

As we prepared to go out for our final dinner together, I heard back from Kathleen and Henry in rapid succession with essentially the same message: thanks, and get that DNA!

From: Kathleen McHugh
To: Me, Henry Fetta, Louise Bier

Angie,
Fabulous research! No surprises! I am thrilled that there are relatives that we can ask to confirm or deny our suspicions. Let's go for it!

Henry, Molly [Kathleen's sister] and I went yesterday to Saint Francis Xavier. Father Joseph is buried there, interestingly enough. We met the secretary for the church. She opened the church up to us and believe it or not, they actually had a museum inside the school which had been closed, celebrating the 175-year history of the church. We went through about an hour's worth of photos and paperwork. I will start sending you some of the information we discovered. Really, not much. Same photos, some financial statements, but nothing revealing. Robin took Henry's phone number because there is a parishioner who has a seven-generation history with the church. I believe she was open to contacting us.

And on another revealing note, we met with Kathleen Brummel/O'Regan [Kathleen was a girl when Ginny came to stay with her family during her pregnancy with Kathleen.] We showed her the picture of Father Ed and her only statement was, "What a nice photograph." However, when I showed her the picture of Father Joseph, she actually screamed in excitement, "Oh my God, that is him, oh my God I can't believe it! Oh my God that is him!" She was actually very surprised by her own reaction. It was quite a moment.
Do you want us to contact these nephews? Time to put this baby to rest.
Henry and I are so lucky to have you both as our cousins. I can't thank you enough for all you've done. So glad you enjoyed Nashville!
Love,

Kathleen

I have to admit that I was a little bit jealous of their trip Saint Francis Xavier church, but it was appropriate that they had the time together, alone. Just as they visited Ginny's grave together, so too they visited Father Joseph's with just each other. I wish I could have been there to see their responses. Were they tearful? Curious? Angry? I would wait and make the trip on my own to the spot where Father Joseph Bier chose to be buried—miles from his childhood home, miles from any family, miles from the places he lived in the thirty years before he actually died. Clearly, St. Francis Xavier in Brighton, Wisconsin, had a hold on his heart. Henry pointed out one additional interesting fact that they gleaned from their visit. While the church is in an unincorporated town called Brighton, its mailing address is in Kansasville—*the same city of residence that Ginny listed for herself on Henry's birth certificate.* Time to put this baby to rest, indeed.

* * *

It took forever for my dad to get his results back. I'm not certain why, but I suspect that he held onto the kit and mulled it over a bit before sending in his sample. Old habits, including suspicion of The Man, die hard. When he received his results, Mom called to discuss the various privacy settings offered. She didn't trust the internet, and assumed that the Russian interference in the 2016 election had something to do with her own email account. She also assumed that the reason that their data usage went up around the holidays had something to do with hackers, rather than the influx of people visiting and logging on to their Wi-Fi. Despite her reservations, I convinced her to make Dad's results public. So, a couple of weeks after the Nashville Genetics summit, we got 'em.

I logged in to 23andme, and there was my dad, listed as my closest relative, up at the top of my list. Tom Bier, with a textbook 50.0% shared DNA. I ran a comparison between him and Kathleen, eager to see how the results matched up with the predictions that Louise and I generated. 23andme reported that Dad and Kathleen shared 10.1% of their DNA. This matched the 10% Louise and I predicted using PopLink, in the scenarios in which Father Ed was NOT their father.

Of course, 23andme interpreted the 10% results in a much simpler manner and labeled my dad and Kathleen as first cousins. In reality, Dad and Kathleen shared that much DNA, not because they were first cousins, but because they were related two ways—through the coincidence of their shared Bier-ness and Roethle-ness. I was reminded of the dangers of drawing conclusions based solely on the results from 23andme. Imagine if Kathleen got these results first. Knowing nothing else, seeing my dad listed as her first cousin would have pointed her down a completely different, largely wrong path. She would have looked among my dad's aunts and uncles for one or other of her biological parents. She wouldn't have latched onto Barb and Liz, quickly tagged Ginny as her mother. Thanks heavens my father guarded his genetic secrets so closely and never even considered 23andme before I suggested (forced) it!

So, Kathleen, Henry and my dad were related as much as predicted if any of the three brother priests were their father. Including, of course, Father Joseph Bier. Dad, Kathleen, and Henry were not first cousins, despite 23andme's reassurances otherwise. My Great Uncle, Monsignor Ed Bier, was eliminated once and for all.

I waited for this day to come, the day when I could firmly cross him off of the list. While so many clues pointed away from Father Ed to Father Joseph, I wasn't sure until that day. I had weirdly mixed emotions. Of course, I was relieved. That being said, I grew to really love Kathleen and Henry. Part of me hoped that Father Ed was their father. I selfishly wanted them to be MORE related to me, so that I could maintain a firm hold on the relationship. I wasn't that worried, though. I wormed myself into their story so thoroughly at this point, I knew it would be impossible to get rid of me.

Casebook summary

•The only likely father at this point is Father Joseph.

•Contact his living relatives
oNeed to confirm with DNA
oNeed to get more information...was he a scoundrel???

Potential Fathers

~~Edward Bier~~
~~Robert Gassert~~
Robert Bier—highly unlikely, unable to prove via genetics
**Joseph Bier
Francis Bier—highly unlikely, unable to prove via genetics
~~Charles Bier~~
~~Raymond Parr~~

Chapter Eighteen
Joseph's Nieces

For some genealogists, recording names and dates is the end game. That sort of researcher would stop with the linking of Ginny Roethle's and Joseph's Bier's names and dates, with the addition of Henry Fetta and Kathleen LeFranc to the tree. They would move on the next question, chasing down the next birth certificate or census document. My voyeuristic instincts needed more. Though we sketched the rough story of Kathleen's and Henry's conceptions and births, we lacked the details and shading to soften those harsh lines. There must have been more to the story than "priest got his housekeeper pregnant—twice." He had to be more than just a scoundrel, if for no other reason than Henry's need for a love story. She had to be more than an unwitting victim, if for no other reason than Ginny's fiery personality, reflected in Kathleen. The next step was obvious. I needed to contact someone from the Father Joseph Bier branch of the Bier family tree. And so, after securing Henry and Kathleen's blessing, I went for it.

My genealogy contact sheet included two people from that branch, also descended from the original Valentine Ten. Valentine and Katherine Bier begat the Ten. One of the Ten was Frank Bier (NOT mystery Frank Bier. This Frank Bier had nothing to do with the Parrs, and everything to do with startling cheekbones.) Frank Bier married Mary Klein. Frank and Mary Bier raised eight children. Three of these children were the brother priests: Fathers Bob, Fran, and Joe. Two of the sisters never married. Three of Frank's and Mary Bier's children had families of their own: two sons, whose descendants I had no contact with whatsoever, and a daughter. That daughter married into the name Raddenbach and raised her *own* family of eight.

This gang of Raddenbach kids, then, were Father Joseph's nieces and nephews. Two of the Raddenbachs contacted me through my blog.

We exchanged brief emails about a year previous. One of them, Hugh Raddenbach, seemed to be a jokester and lived up north. The other, Bernadette, hadn't mentioned where she lived, but she was a teacher and seemed to appreciate the historical aspects of my blog. So, I had names, emails, and a vague notion of these people, Father Joe's nearest living relatives. Except for Henry and Kathleen, of course.

It was time to bite the bullet and just send the messages. But how? I needed to tread lightly, but also cut to the chase. I hemmed and hawed, reflecting on my own response to Liz's and Kathleen's initial inquiry into my own great-uncle priest. I was protective, defensive, and irritated. How would Hugh and Bernadette respond? After all, Father Joseph was their uncle.

What could I possibly write to deliver this news? "Dear Bernadette & Hugh, Were you hoping for some more cousins? Well, you've got 'em! . . ." "Dear Bernadette & Hugh, I'm writing today with shocking news. . ." "Dear Bernadette & Hugh, Have your family get-togethers grown stale? Well, have I got a doozy for you . . ."? Eventually, I struck a reasonable balance, ran my draft by Louise, made a few adjustments, and sent it off.

From: Me
To: Bernadette (Raddenbach) Link, Hugh Raddenbach

Hi Bernadette & Hugh,

This is Angie Bier, the blog person that you corresponded with briefly over the winter. I've been very delinquent in my blogging this summer; it's hard when the kids are home for the summer to have anything resembling a normal routine. We've also been doing quite a bit of traveling this summer, although not back to Germany or the Czech Republic.

I have a somewhat touchy question to pursue...

About a year ago, while I was in Germany, I was contacted by a woman who was adopted back in 1951 and raised in Chicago. She'd figured out that her birth mother was Virginia Roethle. The Roethle family had two marriages with the Biers; one was my great-grandma. So, I was related to her that way. The search for her biological father has taken many twists and turns over the past year. Long story short, we determined that I was related to her ANOTHER way, too—through the Bier side. Many more twists and turns ensued, but at this point, we have a strong suspicion that her father may have been Father Joe Bier.

Her name is Kathleen McHugh, she lives in California now, and she's become a friend. When Kathleen first contacted me, she wondered if her father might have been my own great uncle, Father Ed Bier, but we've since ruled out that possibility. I know that I was floored with tons of mixed emotions when she first contacted me, so believe me, I understand if you're feeling gobsmacked or even angry right now. That being said, I wonder if either of you might be willing to discuss the possibility, given what you knew of him? Either way, I'd still love to meet any or all of you, regardless of the topics on the table.

All the best,
Angie

I anxiously awaited any response. Within an hour or so, I had one—a brief message from Bernadette. She wrote more extensively later that evening. Bernadette, who went by Betty, sent my message on to her sister, Kathy. To try and keep things simple (too late!), I always refer to Kathleen LeFranc as "Kathleen" and Kathy (Raddenbach) Witzack as "Kathy." Hugh never responded—he was on a fishing trip at the time.

From: Bernadette Link
To: Me

Angie
I will respond when at my computer. Good to hear from you- I am not gobsmacked.

Betty

[Later]

From: Bernadette Link
To: Me, Kathy Witzack

Hi All,

Father Joe, as we knew him, was a fairly frequent visitor to our large family farm. He surely loved his little sister, my mom - Veronica, and came for family events, maybe 3 times a year, from my recollection as a child, so could be far off there. When I was first married and living in Milwaukee I was asked by my mom to go visit him in his hospital bed in a "hospice-type" care center in Milwaukee where he was dying of cancer, not sure, but it might have been liver cancer or cirrhosis, as I heard this facility described as a home for "retired" priests, but also alcoholic priests. He was not able to talk long - mostly reminisced about my mom and our home, my family's health, etc. No deathbed confession of having a child, but I wouldn't be the one he would confide in.

He was a jovial man, but definitely a heavy drinker, considering I did not often see my parents consume alcohol unless it was a party, a baptism or confirmation or wedding. It was a bit of a novelty for us. I do remember Father Bob [Father Joe's brother] carried his own suitcase with liquor in it, as I carried it into the farmhouse at one time. Both of these uncles, the ones we knew best, often had housekeepers with them when they visited. Father Bob had the same woman (Kathy may remember her name or I can ask my brother Jim) with him for years. We as older children often speculated about their relationship, but it was a bit taboo to even suggest impropriety.

There would not be surprise on my part at all to hear any priest fathered children - after teaching history for years and reading many novels of the church's role in history and the more recent exposure of pedophilia in the news, it almost seems to have been a given. Certainly condoned - as there are many stories of popes having children.

That's my two cents worth for now. I would enjoy meeting you, Angela. . . I salute your studies and appreciate the info. We have a farm in Viroqua where I could host Hugh from up north further and Kathy and you, maybe Jim would come too - the eldest of our siblings, but not on FB or email. We may travel down to Kathy's some time this fall - which would be more convenient for you, I imagine.

Warmly,
Betty Link (Bernadette)

It was better than I could have hoped for. Betty was open to talking, and the existence of Kathleen did not totally shatter her view of the world. Of course, my initial message didn't yet mention Henry. Her sister, Kathy, was friendly, but much more shocked. She responded in breathless, mind-whirling snippets throughout the day. I later learned that part of her aghast response was due to a misunderstanding of Ginny's age when she first went to live with Father Joseph. Kathy thought she was only 14, but she was actually almost 20. Her train-of-thought responses are best represented as a compendium.

From: Kathy Witzack
To: Me

Angie,
I would be willing and anxious to share what I know about "Father Joe" whenever we can meet. . .

Father Joe (my uncle) had a housekeeper named Ginny! . . .

[After I confirmed that we assumed that the Ginny's were one and the same]

I am anxious to talk to you. I live just west of Janesville. I drive by Grandma Bier's [Mary Bier, wife of Frank] house in Janesville frequently and remember sitting on the front porch swing with her. Shelling sweet peas with her by the garden behind the house and walking to St. Mary's church for mass every morning. . ..

[After I sent a picture of Henry, forgetting that I hadn't yet mentioned him]

What?! They look so alike . . .who is Henry Fetta? . . .

[After I revealed the existence of two children]

OMG, they look so much alike, I can't believe it!!! That's Fr. Joe's son?

Kathy

It turned out that Kathy Witzack, Father Joe's niece, lived about 30 minutes west of my parents' house. Her husband had been in my mother's high school class. Given that my folks' place was a good central meeting spot, we arranged to gather there in about a month's time. Henry would free up his schedule, and Betty would also come into town to visit with her sister and join in. Kathleen was disappointed to be "stuck" in California, but secured promises from her brother and me for frequent updates and pictures. I was relieved that I would see Henry soon. He had been pretty quiet on the email front, ever since I summarized the Nashville Genetics Summit. I hoped he was doing okay.

Over the weeks before the meeting, Betty spread the word of newfound cousins among her siblings. She was one of the youngest, but seemed to fill the role of "organizer" for the family. They all processed the information in different ways. The oldest of the clan was named Jim, and was closest to Father Joe. I talked to him for a few minutes one morning. In the brief time that we chatted, I began to sketch out an image of the Father Joe that the Raddenbach kids knew. He also mentioned that Father Joe wrote an autobiography in verse that it was not to be read by anyone until "after he'd gone." Unfortunately, neither Jim nor anyone else knew what became of this document. Jim longed to get his hands on a copy. After hearing about it, so did I.

None of the Raddenbach kids knew what happened to Father Joe's belongings when he died. The Archdiocese was the last hope. I suspected that the search would be fruitless, given my previous correspondence with the Archdiocese of Milwaukee on the career of Father Joseph Bier. Nevertheless, I again wrote the archivist, requesting any papers or additional information. Once again, she reassured me that they had nothing else in his file. I asked if I could I make an appointment to review his records. The archivist demurred, requesting a specific research question. I demurred back. What would the Archdiocese of Milwaukee have to say about the story that was unfolding? Best to fly low under the radar.

* * *

The meeting of the cousins was scheduled for a Friday at the end of August, when the whine of cicadas on the Rock Prairie rises to deafening levels and the sun takes on that warm glow promising autumn. Attendees would be me, my mom, Henry, Kathy (Raddenbach) Witzack and Betty (Raddenbach) Link. My dad had baseball games to umpire, and Kathleen couldn't make any more trips back from California that summer. My girls would also be there and would stay out of our hair, thanks to the many distractions of Grandma's house and yard. I arrived early to my parents' place, traveling genealogy show in hand. Mom put together a lovely meal for the get-together. It featured a labeled cheese tray, as any good Wisconsin gathering should. I made a panzanella salad, and she contributed several desserts. We decided to set up the meal on the sun porch, which had three walls of screen windows. I figured that if anyone became uncomfortable with the conversation, they could distract themselves by looking out a window at the distant horizon lines. While the country setting was picturesque, it had a major strike against it too: really, really bad internet. Kathleen would not be Skyping in.

Henry arrived first. He parked at the end of my parents' driveway, next to the rusting pickup and the soybean field, barely tinged yellow. The cicadas were riotous, and we chatted over them for a bit after exchanging a hug before heading inside. A few minutes later, Kathy Witzack and Betty pulled up, and we trooped back outside to greet them. Betty was clearly the more extroverted of the two, and both came bearing homemade treats, the social lubricants of the Midwest. Kathy made a salmon salad and some blackberry jam, and Betty had fresh-pressed cider from her orchard up near the Wisconsin River. That day, we ate well.

The group shuffled somewhat awkwardly, until we eventually settled around the table, filled our plates, sipped the icy cider, and got to talking. During a lag in the conversation, with an unspoken nod of agreement, Henry and I launched into a tag-team-telling of their story. I was reminded anew of just how shocking and fresh all this information was for Henry. He only began to learn about the existence of his biological family *three months previous*. In addition to meeting a sister, he was bombarded with cousins, family trees, and the revelation that his father was a priest. Maybe we should have served something stronger than lemonade and cider.

Kathy Witzack and Betty nodded and gasped in all the right places. Betty was seated next to me, and our side of the table tended to dominate the conversation. Kathy Witzack and Henry made the thoughtful comments of natural introverts, and my mother garnished the conversation with lighthearted observations and encouragement to eat more cheese. Things were going well.

And then, we began to question Kathy and Betty. Slowly, an image of the Frank and Mary Bier family began to emerge. Frank Bier and Mary Klein married relatively late in life. He was 25 and she was 32. Interestingly, Mary Klein actually wanted to pursue a religious life herself but felt precluded from doing so because her mother was a Lutheran. Mary wrote,

[A friend] became a Dominican nun, she was 23 when she joined she wanted me to be a nun. Perhaps I would have gone with her, but I had my mother to take care of. She being a Protestant I thought I shouldn't be a nun. Father Roche [the pastor at St. Mary's, Janesville] advised me to get married if I could find a good Catholic who could support me and so I did and he surely was a good husband. He was a railroad man and was sober, pious, and industrious. We had seven children. [Mary does not include their adopted son, Matthew (Beskar) Bier. He was adopted at age 13, having met the family when his orphanage choir sang at Father Bob Bier's first mass] He paid for three boys through seminary to become priests. We did not force them. It was their wish so Daddy and I helped. Our girls all three went to Catholic High school. Veronica [Raddenbach—Betty & Kathy's mother] our youngest to Edgewood Madison.

Shortly before their marriage, Frank began working for the Chicago Northwest Railroad, eager to leave Valentine's farm behind. The newlyweds briefly lived in Chicago, but quickly returned to the familiarity of Janesville, and their home parish of St. Mary's. Mary attended mass *at least* once a day, except if she was indisposed, having children. Frank died in 1945 at age 66. Mary lived to 98, eventually dying almost 25 years later. She continued attending daily mass up until the end.

Their first four children were boys, and three became priests. The second oldest, Charles, married, and he and his wife adopted two children and seemed to quickly lose touch with the rest of the family. The three priests were Father Bob, Father Fran, and Father Joe. Following their ordinations, that was the only way that Mary ever referred to them, never forgetting to include the title "Father." All three attended seminary at St. Francis in Milwaukee, and they all served out their careers at parishes throughout the Archdiocese of Milwaukee.

Father Bob and Father Joe were close to the Raddenbach family, getting together several times per year, both arriving to their sister's farm with housekeepers and liquor in tow. The other priest brother, Father Fran, was remembered to be very intelligent, but not particularly close to the rest of the family. He rarely made the trip back from any of his parish assignments to attend family get-togethers. He spoke four or five different languages and had a creative way of getting in practice. In his free time, he drove down to Milwaukee's industrial harbor and boarded ships arriving from foreign ports, seeking out their captains to practice conversing with native speakers. Betty recalled that Father Fran did attend her brother, Jim's, wedding. In fact, he co-celebrated it with Father Joe, and all they did was argue the entire time—even during the mass itself. Father Bob, while a more frequent family visitor, didn't sound to be a real walk in the park either. He was reportedly a "big John Bircher," a rabble-rouser, and was known to launch into lengthy political diatribes with little provocation.

Betty and Kathy Witzack recalled Father Joe in much the same way that their brother, Jim, had. He was loud, he was boisterous, he loved his sister and her family, he loved being around the kids. He wrote poetry in his free time. Ginny was with him for many years. Betty "wondered" about what was going on there, but the relationship was never openly questioned by anyone in the Raddenbach family. It was the 1950s. Those types of questions were simply never asked.

And what about Frank's and Mary Bier's daughters? The two oldest girls, Agnes and Mary, did not fare well. Both were sent to the convent after graduating eighth grade; neither became a nun. Mary succumbed to some form of mental illness so violent and severe that she required institutional care for the rest of her life. As children, Kathy Witzack and Betty didn't even know that their Aunt Mary existed.

Agnes, too, somehow broke during her time at the convent. She was able to live with her mother for the rest of her life. However, Agnes was extremely anxious and high-strung. Betty recalled that she constantly chewed on celery. Unlike her older sisters, after eighth grade, Veronica went to a Catholic high school and college rather than a convent. She married Jerome "Jerry" Raddenbach and mothered Frank's and Mary

Bier's only biological grandchildren. At least, the only biological grandchildren that they knew of.

The youngest of Frank's and Mary Bier's kids was Matthew, a son adopted at age 13. Mary forgot to count him in her diary, and Betty actually forgot to mention him in an early email reviewing the genealogy of the Frank and Mary Bier family. I wasn't sure how much to read into this. When I asked about his omission, both Kathy and Betty explained that it was unintentional and that there were no hard feelings between the families. Perhaps his omission was an oversight, perhaps his adoption at such an old age—13—caused him to be thought of somewhat differently by the family. I later learned that he and his brother grew up in an orphanage on the grounds of St. Francis Seminary. The year he was adopted, the orphanage burned down and the orphan boys were either fostered or adopted out.

Betty and Kathy reminisced fondly about their Grandmother Mary, their visits to the big white farmhouse, walking to mass every day. Mary lived with her daughter, Agnes, and Agnes was often in charge of the grandkids' bedtime routine, a cup of cocoa with a splash of brandy, kneel for a rosary, and off to bed.

When Veronica and Jerry Raddenbach eventually died and Betty was settling her parents' estate, she came across Mary Bier's diaries. Mary recorded the events of important days, also noting when someone offered her a ride home from daily mass. She mentioned that Father Bob had a nervous breakdown at one point. She frequently wrote of the "Fathers," and noted that two of her daughters "went to be nuns." She hoped that one of her grandkids would pursue a religious life (none did).

When we looked up from our scraped-clean plates, dessert having long since passed, several hours had passed. As we talked, we tried to imagine these two people's lives and their motivations: Joe and Ginny, Ginny and Joe. Both came from intensely Catholic families. Both families held Father Charles Bier, the original Bier priest, in high esteem. Both of their mothers were widowed at a relatively young age and likely saw the convent as a convenient way to settle their daughters with little expense. Sending the three Bier brothers to seminary was expensive, as Mary's diary entry suggests. Religious life didn't stick for Ginny, or either of Father Joe's sisters. Ginny abandoned religious life completely, and Father Joe pursued an illegitimate version of it.

"It's really amazing," I said weighing my words, "that religion, something that could bring so much comfort, could at the same time seemingly cause so much harm. I mean, look at those diaries. Mary's faith truly sustained her. And you, Mom, I've never met someone who so truly loves their church and their faith like you."

"Yes, I love my church family, but some things about The Church," she replied, motioning to indicate the larger church body, "I just don't know. It just seems so unfair that our priests can't get married. When you look at it, there just isn't that strong of a theological argument for why priests can't marry and have children. But I'm beginning to think it's just not going to change in my lifetime." She shook her head and started clearing plates.

"Although," Kathy said, "Pope Francis is at least trying to move things in the right direction."

We talked about some of my mom's frustrations with the Diocese of Madison, including the bishop's refusal to waste resources in the ordination of deacons, a formal position that can be held by non-ordained men. This was a vocation that my father long hoped to pursue during his retirement, but his request was refused.

"Oh, what a shame," said Henry. "That is such a special process. In fact, just last weekend, I went to the ordination to the deaconate of a very good friend of mine. The Archdiocese of Chicago doesn't seem to be having those problems."

I wondered where Henry was with his faith journey, and this gave me a good idea that he remained devout. I tailored my next words accordingly. I watched him and Mom, the practicing Catholics, and they nodded as I continued.

"Ginny and Father Joe had so much in common. Both were from very devout families, both sent to pursue the religious life, perhaps a bit against their will," I said. "Mary says that all three boys chose that life for themselves, but there must have been SOME pressure. After all, most families of eight don't produce one priest, let alone eight!" I said, picking up steam. "And then, they met. And maybe both somehow wished for a life that they couldn't have, and boom, they found each other, someone who truly could understand their situation.

"There was Ginny, who was essentially exiled for rejecting the convent. She was 19 and, by all accounts, beautiful and vivacious. And she was sent away from her family and friends to serve as a housekeeper for her second cousin, whom she probably barely knew, in a rural, isolated parish. She must have been lonely and confused and more than a little bitter.

"And then you have Father Joseph," I continued. "It's impossible to look into his mind and determine his personal enthusiasm for a religious life. However, we know that the superiority of the priesthood above all else was pounded into his and his siblings' minds from a young age.

"So, overlooking the obvious power imbalances that existed between the two, might they have formed some sort of a bond around the shared identity of living out a religious fantasy life created by their parents? Specifically, a life that expressly forbade romantic love with a life partner? I don't know if we can say that it was true love, or even healthy love, but for the two of them, maybe this secret, broken version of love was the closest that either of them would ever have. It might have been broken, but maybe it was the best that either of them could ever hope for."

I ended my monologue with an emotional shrug and eyebrow raise, and looked around the table. Everyone nodded slightly, digesting my words. I so desperately wanted to give Henry the gift of some sort of a love story. This was the best, the most honest that I could do.

Unsurprisingly, their broken bond did not last. Joe and Ginny lived under the same roof at St. Francis Xavier for nine years, and then for some time together at Father Joseph's next parish in Fond du Lac, a city much farther to the north. After Fond du Lac, he was briefly at the parish that was the home of the scandal with *another* housekeeper, the pamphlets, the litigation. After that, he abruptly retired. Where was Ginny in all this? How did they end up separated, buried miles apart? We would likely never know. Relationships forged in the healthiest environments often fracture.

As we got up from the table, Betty looked at Henry.

"Well, can we make it official? Do you feel like everything fits well enough together to officially declare yourself our cousin?" Betty laughed as she said it.

I understood her feeling. Hallmark doesn't create announcements for the occasion of certifying one's previously hidden birth story. "We are proud to announce the addition of two new cousins to our family. Through a combination of DNA, genealogy, and good old-fashioned gumshoeing, we're declaring Joseph Bier and Virginia Roethle to have been the biological parents of Henry Fetta and Kathleen LeFranc." Even so, a declaration was necessary. I knew that Henry's response meant everything in terms of framing the relationship.

Henry flashed Betty and Kathy a patented, gentle-Henry smile. "Yes, yes I think we can," he said. And later, Kathleen, who I was surreptitiously texting the entire time, agreed, with patented Kathleen emojis and exclamation marks. We shared this final exchange with Betty and Kathy, who were happy to receive it.

As we gathered in the driveway to say goodbye, I had to ask Henry one more question. Over the course of the day, some of our views on the Catholic church were laid bare. My mom loved it unconditionally, despite recognizing its challenges. Betty, I believe, left it entirely. I converted to the Episcopal church. I wasn't sure about Kathy. Henry remained beatifically quiet. So, I just blurted it out.

"Henry, what has this whole thing done to your faith?" I asked, in typically direct fashion.

"It's as strong as ever," he said, with a peaceful smile in the setting sunlight.

Oh, Joe and Ginny, Ginny and Joe. How I wished you could know how well your children turned out.

Casebook summary

•It's as official as it can be. Case closed?

Potential Fathers

~~Edward Bier~~
~~Robert Gassert~~
~~Robert Bier~~
Joseph Bier
~~Francis Bier~~
~~Charles Bier~~
~~Raymond Parr~~

Chapter Nineteen
Welcome Home

St. Francis Xavier Church was only a 30-minute drive south of my home, but I didn't visit until Henry invited me. He and Kathleen dropped by the day after the Roethle Reunion. They found Father Joseph's grave, and they connected with some parish members. That day, Father Joseph's being their father was still only a strong possibility, not yet confirmed. As such, they declined to reveal the details of their story, choosing instead to label him an uncle. Afterward, Henry remained in touch with a woman named Marilyn who ran the parish museum. She suggested he visit during the yearly parish festival in the fall to learn more about his "uncle." That way, there'd be a greater chance of meeting older parishioners who might remember Father Joe.

The weekend of the festival, which included a Turkey Supper, was in early November. I requested a non-highway route from the GPS. This circuitous approach was long and unfamiliar. Perhaps I only felt I was spiraling further and further into the middle of nowhere. Realistically, though, St. Francis Xavier *was* in the middle of nowhere. Aside from the church building and adjacent cemetery, the town of Brighton consisted of a half-dozen houses loosely gathered together, and a tavern called Jeddy's.

I drove into town at noon on a Sunday, and Jeddy's was already hopping. It was a football Sunday in Wisconsin. More surprising than the traffic at Jeddy's was the traffic at the church. St. Francis Xavier was the epitome of a country church—traditionally shaped with a tall steeple and arched, stained glass windows marching down its length. The facade glowed in the drizzly November drear. It was clad in Cream City Brick, a buttery white brick unique to Milwaukee. A small hill gently rolled away to the south of the church, dotted with headstones. To the north stood a solidly square house in need of a facelift. Was this the rectory where Father Joe and Ginny lived? A small parking lot was attended by several men in ponchos. It was packed with cars, as was a pasture adjacent to the cemetery. An additional 50 or so cars lined both sides of the country road. Given the unpopulated surroundings, I couldn't begin to fathom where all the cars came from.

I pulled into an open spot on the shoulder and texted Henry. He was already in the parish hall, a small building that might have once been a school. I opened my door and an umbrella and cold spray of rain battered me. I wouldn't be spending any leisure time in the cemetery grounds that day. I hurried, head down, towards the hall. I quickly realized that my green dress and ankle boots made me far overdressed for the occasion. Most of the other attendees sported their Packer best, jeans and a green and gold top of some variety.

As I stepped inside, I was greeted by warmth, the smell of turkey, and several volunteers with blue nametags. To the left hung a row of eight-by-ten, black and white photographs of previous parish priests. Father Joseph was quickly recognizable in the second oldest photo. It was the same photograph that we all had copies of already, the one from his obituary. I scanned the hallway and quickly spotted Henry. We stowed our umbrellas on the rack above the navel-height coat hooks, and he explained that no one else from his family was able to join us. Illness and previous engagements kept them away. As always, Henry had a calm, welcoming demeanor. I imagine that it masked a degree of nervousness, though. After all, he was visiting the only real home that his birth parents ever shared. I asked him what our "play" was.

"I've spoken to Marilyn and told her that I'm a nephew of Father Joseph's, and that's about as far as I've taken it," Henry replied.

"Do you think we should tell anyone the truth?" I asked.

"Well, yes, of course, but let's just see how things progress."

"I'll follow your lead," I said.

I followed Henry to a doorway marked "Museum of Faith." We stepped inside a former classroom lined with tables and displays. My archivist heart did a leap. Inside were all the treasures, ephemera, and documents of the church's 175+ year history, carefully displayed and explained with accompanying placards. It was a marvelous space, and I learned that the vast majority of the work was undertaken by a few dedicated volunteers. It was like watching my future flash before my eyes.

As I greedily scanned the treasure-trove of a room, Henry addressed three women standing inside the door. "Excuse me, but do any of you know Marilyn?"

The two on the outside took a step back, and the woman in the middle said, "You must be Henry!" She gave him a brief hug, squishing her black fanny pack in the process. The other two women slipped away as introductions were made. She then led us into the museum space.

Marilyn told us about a 90-year old "sharp as a tack" parishioner, the living historian of the place. Unfortunately, she was traveling. Marilyn, however, made sure to borrow one of the lady's scrapbooks, the one that covered the years of Father Joseph's tenure. While I gushed over the amazing space, Henry reverently approached the scrapbook. It was open to a page with a typewritten sheet summarizing Father Joseph's time at the parish, 1951-1960. At the top was a snapshot of him working at a typewriter. It was taken in ¾ profile, and he wasn't looking at the camera. However, his distinctive nose and chin were clearly outlined. Save for the fact that Henry still bore a healthy head of hair, the resemblance was striking. I was amazed that Marilyn didn't comment on it. There were about ten more pages of information, including several newspaper clippings and some photographs, including a large black and white of the rectory in its former glory. Marilyn promised to make copies for us, but first, she wanted to introduce us. She said that "a bunch" of people were anxious to meet us. Apparently, we were expected.

Marilyn led us into another former classroom. A line snaked in through one door, and guests bought tickets for dinner, beers, and a raffle for a combination grill and smoker. She took us to a short, older man with a prominent belly and teeth worn to stubs who she introduced as Paul. Shaking hands with us, Paul said, "Oh, yeah, I knew Father Bier. He baptized a lot of our children." Throughout our exchange, the broad grin never left his face. He was married around the same time that Father Joe came to Saint Francis Xavier, and Father Bier was in charge of the parish during the early years of Paul's family. He ran a dairy operation just around the corner and was a font of information on the history of the church, which he reminded us predated that of the Archdiocese of Milwaukee.

It was difficult to keep him on track, and I soon realized that Paul was the type of person who enjoyed recounting facts and figures, rather than personal reminiscences. So, I steered the conversation to the founding of the church. We learned that it was originally settled by Irish immigrants. In the late 1800s, the population began to skew to majority German, as did that of the rest of the greater Milwaukee area. The Cream City brick structure was not the original church. Paul was excited to relate that the original wooden building was destroyed by a cyclone, which picked it up and unceremoniously dropped it in a field across the street. When the new church was built, the Irish and the Germans couldn't agree on a name; the Irish wanted St. Patrick's, the Germans St. Boniface. The pastor at the time ended the argument by instead naming it after himself and his own patron saint: St. Francis Xavier. The historical discord was recorded for all posterity in the placement of the stained-glass windows. Those donated by Irish families commemorated St. Patrick and reside on one side of the church, and the Germans' St. Boniface windows stare them down from across the aisle.

Henry assessed Paul's familiarity with genetic testing. He chatted about family history and genealogy, then asked if he'd ever heard of 23andme. Not surprisingly, Paul didn't take the bait. However, another slightly younger man named Len was familiar.

Len joined us midway through the conversation. Len appeared about 20 years younger than Paul, but it turned out he was in his 70s, only a handful of years younger than Paul. Len knew Father Joseph as his Saturday catechism instructor and described him with one word:

"Tough." Len went on, "Yeah, he stayed over there in the rectory with Ginny. They took care of the gardens together and he mowed the cemetery. He's buried there, you know," he added.

"That's so interesting," I replied. "Why would he choose this parish to be buried at, rather than with his family, or wherever he was when he died?"

"Well, I dunno, but it's a pretty spot," Len replied and I agreed.

"So, you knew Ginny?" Henry asked.

"Yeah, Ginny. She was around and in the church all the time."

I tried to restrain my prying interest, and I failed. "Was anyone else in and out of the rectory during those years? Say, an associate pastor? Groundskeeper?" I asked

"Nope, just them," Len replied. "But then when the airfield went up, Father Bier'd invite the ranking military guys over to play craps. And he really liked Jeddy's."

Apparently, little changed in the Brighton crossroads in 70 years.

I felt it was a sign that Len spontaneously brought up Ginny, remembered her name, and sharing that he often saw Father Joe and her working side by side. I hoped that he would be a good person to hear the truth. I needed to tell someone and test their response. Len stepped away to talk to another friend, and Marilyn was bringing in another older parishioner to meet Henry.

"Henry," I interrupted Paul, "I'm going to go *talk to Len*," I said, with awkward intensity and dramatic eyebrow raises. "Do you think it's okay to *talk to Len?*" I wanted to follow his lead, after all. Henry tipped his head. I was certain that I was just given the okay to proceed.

Perhaps Henry mentally rehearsed such a conversation, but I had not. How should I approach this? How would Len respond? In typical fashion, I leapt right in. "Hey, Len," I interrupted his conversation and put a hand on his arm, "Um, I wanted to tell you something about Henry over there."

He smiled at me with a slightly quizzical look on his face.

"You know how he was saying that he's related to Father Bier? Actually, Henry was adopted when he was a baby, and we're about as sure as we can be that Father Joe was his biological father," I said.

Len's eyes actually bugged out. He leaned in, interested.

I continued. "And that Ginny was his mother. And Henry has a full biological sister that he just met a few months ago. We're pretty sure that Father Joe and Ginny had two kids and gave them both up for adoption, both while they were here at St. Francis Xavier."

I paused for breath, and John said, "Wow. That's amazing. Huh." His body language was interested, not defensive.

"What do you think about that?"

I don't recall his exact words, but they amounted to: "You never know what people are up to, and we've learned a lot about the lives of priests in the Catholic church since I was a kid."

Relieved, I reassured Len that we weren't trying to make waves, that Henry wanted to talk to some people who actually knew Father Joe and Ginny.

Len said that he had no intention of talking about the story with anyone else, and thanked me for sharing with him. As the conversation was winding up, he grew thoughtful. "You know, I had an aunt who served lunches at the school that they built," Len said. "And Ginny would sometimes come over and help her. And one time, I was there at the house, and my uncle and aunt were talking about Ginny. And my uncle, he said, 'he [Father Bier] has got her so she'll always stay with him,' you know, implying something sexual. My aunt just shushed him up. In those days, you didn't discuss things like that. But I guess my uncle was right," Len said.

While I talked with Len, Henry chatted with several other parishioners who knew Father Joe. He was remembered fondly. Father Joe was tough in class, but always found time to pitch for the kids' softball games. He liked to go ice skating on the pond in winter. And, if they remembered Ginny, they remembered that she and Father Joe always worked together, side by side. No one, though, remembered Ginny being away for months at a time.

Paul, the old man with whom we originally spoke, recalled that he wasn't able to attend Father Joe's funeral. It was held in Milwaukee, and then his casket was brought to Brighton for burial in the parish cemetery. Paul was around on the day of the burial and mentioned his disappointment to the funeral director, who said he'd allow him to have a private viewing. "And he opened up the casket, right there, and I said a little prayer. That's the only time that's ever happened to me," said Paul.

I again pondered the significance of Father Joe choosing this lonely country cemetery as his final resting place. Was it an indication that he treasured his memories of this place above all others? I glanced over Henry's shoulder. There, next to the egg-shaped grill up for raffle, stood a priest. This must be the pastor of Saint Francis. I read his brief bio on the church's website, and so I knew in advance an interesting fact about him; he was married.

In 1980, Pope John Paul II made a path to ordination for married priests converting to Roman Catholicism from the Anglican or Episcopal Churches, in which celibacy is not required of clergy (8). There were about 125 such married Roman Catholic priests in the United States. The pastor of St. Francis Xavier was one of them. In what I could only see as a stroke of divine irony, the parish home of Father Joseph and Ginny's clandestine love affair was now home to an openly married priest, serving the parish faithfully for the past eight years.

"Hello," I walked up to the pastor with hand extended. "This is my first time attending this event. I can't believe how big it is."

"Yes. We serve over 2,000 meals. It's quite the undertaking. I'm Father Arnett," the man replied.

"Hi, I'm Angie—Angie Bier. I'm related to Father Joseph Bier, one of your former clergy." I motioned to the pictures in the hallway.

"Ah, yes. Well, welcome."

"Thanks. I'm here with my cousin, Henry. We're interested in learning more about Father Joseph Bier. . . "and then—I told him. I briefly related the story, always careful to include the phrase, "as certain as we can be," and, "we only want to learn more about Father Joe and Ginny, not cause a scandal." Father Arnett's eyebrows creased a bit as I shared the facts of the case, but he made little noises at times, indicating interest and empathy, rather than judgment and defensiveness. I felt that, again, I made the right call.

"And that's about it, really. Henry is a wonderful, devout man. He doesn't want to harm the church's memories of Father Joseph. He just wants to try to form an image of what his biological parents' life was like around the time that he was born. No one in the family seems to know, so here we are," I concluded.

"I see," replied Father Arnett. He chose his words carefully. "Well, you both are certainly welcome. I can't offer much to help with your investigations, but the story certainly seems plausible."

I was relieved by his measured, open response. I introduced Henry to Father Arnett, letting him know that the priest knew the truth of his identity. They briefly chatted about the church, the festival, and the weather, before the conversation broke up, and Henry and I were left alone in each other's company once more.

I found out later that, while I talked to Len and Father Arnett, Henry also revealed the truth to several people. They received it with varying degrees of surprise, but no discernible negative judgment. We paused for Henry to update Kathleen on our group chat of the events so far.

HF: Angie and I have already met several people who remember Fr. Joseph and Ginny, all with fond memories. Before I said anything, four people have said, "You look a lot like Fr. Bier," including the current parish priest, Fr. Russ Arnett. We have shared the story with a few folks, a couple of gasps, but not really surprised as they think about their relationship. Turns out they maintained the cemetery grounds together. A blessing to be here with Angie, more to come.

KL: Oh, my heavens!!! Such a special day! Can't wait to hear more. Hug Angie for me!

Which, of course, he did.

* * *

Before we adjourned to the turkey dinner, Henry said that there was one person that we absolutely needed to speak to before we took another step: Marilyn, the parish historian who helped arrange the whole day. He urgently wanted to apprise her of all that we discovered since his summer visit, especially before any other parishioner might tell her first.

When Henry and I returned to the Museum of Faith, Marilyn was hard at work. Henry placed a hand gently on her arm and said, "Marilyn, before we go any further, there's something I need to tell you. You deserve an explanation." Henry began while Marilyn looked on placidly. "I am actually adopted, and over the past several months, I have been on an amazing journey of faith and discovery. And through the help of several people, including my expert genealogist here," motioning to me, "I found family that I never knew I had. And as amazing as it sounds, we are as certain as we possibly can be that Father Joseph was actually my father, and Ginny, his housekeeper, my mother."

Marilyn glanced between the two of us in stunned silence.

"I didn't want to tell you over the phone," Henry said. "I felt that this was something better done face to face. But I've mentioned it to a couple of people, and I want you to hear it from me first."

Marilyn continued to appear hesitant, so I interrupted. "I want you to know, Marilyn, that Henry wants nothing more than to learn first-hand memories about his birth parents. He doesn't want to cause a scandal or rock the boat. He is a kind, faithful man, and you can trust him."

By this time, Marilyn found her words. "Well, just be careful who you tell," she said. "These are country people, and you know, they can be really judgmental."

Henry expressed his thanks several more times over, and we joined the line for the turkey dinner. By this point, both of our stomachs were audibly rumbling, and we needed a break to unpack all that we learned.

The dinner itself was scrumptious, served up family style in mismatched Pyrex bowls. We exchanged pleasantries with the other people at our table; they were clearly there for the food and not the conversation of strangers. Henry and I talked over what we learned, as well as the questions that still lingered. Had people suspected that Father Joe and Ginny were more than employer and employee? Had anyone known about the pregnancies? How come no one noticed that she was away for months at a time? How did Father Joe and Ginny eventually drift apart? What about the final housekeeper at the parish that led to his early retirement—where was Ginny during all of this? Every time that we felt we learned answers, which we most certainly had, we ended up with a list just as long of new ones.

We cleared our plates and thanked our hosts. I left immediately to pick up the girls, and Henry hung around for a bit, perhaps hoping to win the grill in the raffle. We returned to the November drear and our regular lives, miles removed from the ghostly echoes of this country parish, far removed from prying eyes, natal families, and expectations. When Henry got home, he sent another text to the group chat.

HF: Angie, you are a guardian angel and gift in our lives. Today would not have been the same without you. . . I think parishioners wondered why Fr. Joe and Ginny were both away from the parish at various times and there were suspicions. For two children to have been born to them during their time there is a bit difficult for them to grasp. No one is questioning the validity of the story. We missed your presence.

KL: We are very fortunate to have Angie in our lives. It's overwhelming being accepted by all.

I guess all of my worries about being an unwanted voyeur were baseless. Henry and Kathleen's picture of me didn't match up with the mental version that I carried around of myself. But it felt nice to hear nonetheless.

* * *

The following Monday, I started writing this chapter. I wanted to capture the memories while they were fresh—both for myself, and for Kathleen. When I finished the first several pages, I sent off the draft to her and Henry.

From: Me
To: Kathleen LeFranc, Henry Fetta

Wow, it was an amazing day. I've started to write up my memories of the day. I'm only about a quarter of the way through, but I have to do boring stuff now like LAUNDRY! I wanted to share what I have so that you, Kathleen, can get a sense of what it was like. We missed you soooooooo much.

xoxo
AB

From: Kathleen McHugh
To: Me, Henry Fetta
Oh, my heavens, Angie! You have me in suspense! Get back to work! You write beautifully, woman!

I felt badly that Kathleen, the woman who started this whole thing, missed out on the recent revelations—those of Father Joseph's nieces and nephews, the memories of the parishioners at St. Francis Xavier. So, I finished the chapter for her, the best that I could do, especially after she and Henry kept heaping awkwardness-inducing praise on me.

From: Henry Fetta
To: Me, Kathleen McHugh

Hi, Angie,
I agree with my dear sister, Kathleen, "you write beautifully, woman!" Thanks for putting your reflections into words so quickly.

One unfortunate outcome from the visit is that I received a note from Marilyn, who said she felt "used" and that she did not want to remain in contact. I sent her a note to apologize for any hurt I caused her and to thank her for all she did to connect us with so many parishioners who knew Fr. Joseph and Ginny. I have not heard back. In retrospect, I should have shared our story with her first thing upon my arrival and asked her if she was okay with proceeding.

On the other hand, as I was leaving on Sunday, I took the opportunity to say good-bye and thank Father Arnett. As I was telling him that I view the grounds there as holy land for Kathleen and me, he took my hand and said, "Henry, welcome home, you are always welcome here." My knees almost buckled and he made my ride home one of introspection and reflection on what a blessed few months this has been for us. If only Fr. Joseph and Ginny knew the joy they have brought to our lives.

Thank you again and again, Angie, for being there on Sunday and for being my rock when I needed you to lean on. Let our journeys continue in the most unbelievably interconnected way possible :)
Love, Henry

I was chagrined to hear that Marilyn was hurt. Perhaps her warning about "country people being judgmental" was far more prescient than either of us suspected. I hoped that other parishioners didn't blame her for inviting Henry and me.

We stewed about this hurt for months afterward, him much more than me. We had a couple of phone conversations about it, and I tried to reassure him that forgiveness was needed. We needed to forgive the forces that acted on Father Joseph and Ginny, on the world that they lived in. We needed to forgive Marilyn, and most importantly, Henry needed to forgive himself. We were operating in uncharted territory. His motivations came from an honest place, and any harm he caused was unintentional. I told Henry that I forgave him, and that I hoped he could do the same for himself.

"My wife, Lynn, says the same thing," he replied.

Throughout this entire fraught journey, the only rebuke we received from anyone came from Marilyn, a woman who hadn't even belonged to the parish at the time of Father Joe's tenure. Father Joe's only living relatives, his nieces and nephews, were welcoming and kind, as were Ginny's. Surely they struggled to assimilate these newfound relatives into their mental pictures of Father Joe and Ginny, yet they received Henry and Kathleen with only grace.

The best explanation that I can settle on for Marilyn's response is that we caretakers of the stories—genealogists, amateur historians, and the like—can be quite protective indeed.

St. Francis Xavier Church, Brighton, Wisconsin

Chapter Twenty
Merry Christmas

After our time at St. Francis Xavier, I felt that it was time to turn the page on this story. I helped confirm Kathleen's and Henry's parentage, and did quite a bit of work toward filling in the gaps in the narrative of Father Joseph Bier and his housekeeper / second cousin / lover, Ginny Roethle. The remaining unanswered questions did not require the expertise of either a genealogist or a geneticist. And, as such, my role in the rest of the story would be a decidedly supporting one. It was time to package the whole thing up, give it to Kathleen and Henry and their families, and let the rest of the chips fall where they may. Time for me to exit stage right. I learned many things from my genealogist grandmother, one of them being the significant role of handwritten greeting cards. Somehow, we still didn't have each other's actual addresses.

From: Me
To: Kathleen LeFranc, Henry Fetta
As I go through all of our old correspondence, I realize what an up and down emotional journey that this has been. How are you both feeling as we approach the first holidays with this new family? Either of you planning to add stollen to your Christmas table?

I'd love to send you each a Christmas card. Would you be willing to share your addresses?

xoxo
Angie

Stollen is a traditional German sweet bread, studded with dried fruits and often soaked in brandy. I began experimenting with recipes a few years back. Kathleen and Henry were both raised in Irish Catholic homes, though. I wondered if their newfound German ancestries loomed large that Christmas?

From: Kathleen LeFranc
To: Me, Henry Fetta

Angie,
I'll share mine if you share yours!

PS....do you have a family recipe for Stollen? I'd love it if you do,.... I've eaten, it but never made it. This could be a great year to start a new tradition! It's actually very hard for me to be away, knowing that I have a brother and a new family.
Love you,
Kathleen

From: Henry Fetta
To: Me, Kathleen LeFranc

Hi, Angie and Kathleen,
When I think that less than six months ago, I had no idea what my birth mother's name was and now have an amazingly wonderful extended family, I have to simply revert to this being both a miraculous and magical journey. It's a gift like no other.

Life is always amazing!
Henry

Leave it to Henry to always get back to the heart of the matter. In typical fashion, Kathleen and I focused on the lighthearted matters at hand. In this case? Recipes.

From: Me
To: Kathleen LeFranc, Henry Fetta

We do not have a traditional stollen recipe. As far as I know, the only recipe that survives intact from the Valentine Bier era is one for graupen, (sp?), or pigs blood sausage made with barley! I've never tried it myself. I've started making stollen over the past year or two to establish a new German tradition in our house. We have bibimbap on Christmas Eve, a traditional Korean dish. And then stollen and whatever else I want to make Christmas day. There's also a required suite of Christmas cookies that come down from my Grandma Bier, but I think they only go about as far back as she does . . . Enjoy! Let me know if you have any questions. My favorite is the candy cane cookies—they absolutely must be iced as they're not terribly sweet on their own!

xoxo
AB

From: Kathleen LeFranc
To: Me
Oh, my heavens, Angie! Thank you so very much! That is absolutely amazing that you have all those recipes in your grandmother's handwriting. It's pouring rain here, so a good time to turn on the oven and get to work!

In between baking, shopping, decorating, and all the other tasks to make Christmas "happen", I found time to sneak in one additional gift. That holiday season, 23andme ran a huge ad campaign that featured the Grinch as spokesman, and exhorted consumers to give the gift of family revelation. I bit. We had no DNA from any of Father Joseph's nephews—neither Henry nor Kathleen had gotten around to asking for their spit, perhaps not feeling in a position to do so. So, I contacted one of the nephews, Hugh Raddenbach. He readily agreed to spit for the cause. I ordered a kit to be sent to his northern Wisconsin home, provided some additional instructions via email, and waited.

From: Me
To: Kathleen LeFranc, Henry Fetta

Merry Christmas! My gift to you both is securing one of Father Joseph's nephews to do a 23andme analysis. As I told him, we're as sure as we can be that Father Joe is your father, but it'll be the icing on the cake (or the stollen?) to see him show up as your first cousin. It'll be Hugh Raddenbach, he is brother to Kathy Witzack and Betty Link who we met over the summer.

Xoxo
AB

From: Henry Fetta
To: Me, Kathleen LeFranc

Hi, Angie,
THANK YOU for this wonderful present to Kathleen and me, you are the gift that keeps on giving. As we talked when we were together with Kathy and Betty, it would be wonderful to spend some time with Hugh as it seems like he was the closest nephew to Father Joseph. Maybe we can arrange a rendezvous when Kathleen is next in the Chicago area?

Merry Christmas to you and your family, Henry

Several weeks later, 23andme confirmed that Hugh Raddenbach was Henry and Kathleen's first cousin. Of course, they shared more DNA than a typical first cousin would. Remember that Henry and Kathleen were both Hugh's first cousin by virtue of Father Joe *and* his second-cousins-once-removed by virtue of Ginny.

Confused? At this point, you just have to trust me on this one.

From: Henry Fetta
To: Me

Hi, Angie,
Thanks again for sending Hugh the kit; as expected, we are first cousins, absolutely amazing! The combination of scientific and

empirical evidence has found a brand-new extended family for us, what a blessing.

Now that it's "official" that Father Joseph Bier and Virginia Roethle are Kathleen and my biological parents, I'd like to put a simple family tree together for the LeFranc and Fetta families so that they can see the Bier and Roethle trees and the relationship between Grandma Helen Bier and Fr. Joseph. Is there a simple tool that you would recommend for this? I am hoping to keep it to one/two pages at first and will probably need your help :)

Hope the New Year has begun well for you and your family. So happy to call you cousin :)
xoxo Henry

I laughed out loud when I read Henry's first request. A simple version of this convoluted family tree? The one in which both of their parents were related to Valentine Bier? And the same tree in which both they and I were related to Roethles and Biers by virtue of siblings marrying an uncle and niece? With various intersecting Parrs and other red herrings? And all of the potential priests that we long since eliminated? And all on one page or less? It would take a Christmas miracle.

In the end, with much painful pruning and the judicious use of color-coding, I produced something that proved helpful to my newfound cousins, and everyone else to whom I attempted to relate this confusing story.

From: Me
To: Henry Fetta
Hi, Henry—

Easy family tree.... hmm. I have to laugh at this one, because even a simplified family tree is tricky. The programs that I use for my data management tend to skew comprehensive, not exactly what you were looking for. I have hand-drawn a couple of trees that might help. I'll work on scanning them and get them to you.

Happy New Year!
xoxo
Angie

The tree that I ultimately ended up sending them is the one that has been fleshed out over the course of this book, more or less. I included all of the theoretical priests that were originally possibilities.

From: Henry Fetta
To: Me, Kathleen LeFranc
This is terrific and very helpful, thanks for sending. As I've shared before, I am proud to be number 2141 (I think that's right, but may need to fact check it :)) on your extended family tree.

I just spoke with Hugh Raddenbach who couldn't be kinder and more welcoming. Kathleen, he said he spoke to you earlier in the week and you mentioned a possible May visit. We will have some fun planning time with family and some additional visits in WI whenever you are able to come.

Angie, Kathleen and I spoke briefly about our health and could not be more grateful, we have strong genes and since we're 3/4 Bier, is anyone surprised? :)
Cheers, Henry

From: Kathleen LeFranc
To: Me, Henry Fetta
Angie,
This is great. It's so much easier to be able to have visual aids. Henry, yes, I mentioned to Hugh that I was going to try to come out in May. I need to know with you and Angie if there is a weekend that works best. I remembered that Father Joseph supposedly had a lake house, so I asked Kathy if she remembered the name of the lake, thinking that

might be a nice spot for a reunion, but she didn't. Everyone seems anxious to get together, so I thought I'd start to plan. We can really go anywhere, but first, I need to come up with a date. Help!
Love you both!

While I completed the impossible-to-simplify-very-much-at-all tree for Henry and Kathleen, I addressed his second request: follow up on my get-together with the Raddenbachs. When we met for lunch at my parents' in August, Kathy Witzack and Betty loaned me several of Mary Bier's diaries. I transcribed them and scanned what I needed. I was embarrassed at my delay in getting the artifacts back into the hands of their rightful owners. I asked Kathy whether I could stop by during the week between Christmas and New Year's. I call this "the golden week." All of the pressures of the holidays are off, and my family engages in a days'-long traveling feast, moving from house to house, gathering fluctuating groups of relatives and friends, playing hours of board games, and eating really ridiculous amounts of cheese and cured meats. Since I'd be at my parents' nearby home on more than a few of these days, I figured I could just swing by Kathy's with the diaries whenever she was home.

We settled on a day, and then she proceeded to craft a traveling-feast around my arrival. I invited my mom along as wingman, since she already met Kathy and Betty. Each of their husbands would also be there, as would their brother, Jim Raddenbach, the eldest brother with whom I briefly spoke by phone over the summer. He promised to bring photo albums. Unfortunately, neither Henry nor Kathleen could attend. I felt guiltily-selfish, indulging in this gathering of cousins in their absence.

On the appointed day, I picked up my mom and left my girls with their grandpa, aunts, and uncle for that day's board games and charcuterie. We drove in a wide loop around Janesville to the Witzack house. It was equally in the middle of nowhere, but on the other side of town. Unlike my parents' old brick farmhouse on the windswept prairie, the Witzacks lived in a newer ranch home, nestled in hilly terrain next to a swath of old growth forest. Mom and I admitted to being a little bit nervous, as we weren't quite sure what exactly we'd be walking into.

The Raddenbach family gathering, though, could have blended seamlessly into our own. Kathy served a scrumptious lentil soup and homemade bread on her Christmas china, and we polished off two bottles of Riesling. Chairs were gathered into a loose circle in the cozy living room, and conversational groups formed and re-formed. Mom and the Raddenbach kids found mutual friends from their growing-up years in the Catholic schools of southern Wisconsin. Betty was the natural leader of the group, but the comic relief came from her brother, Jim Raddenbach. His round, balding face was cracked into a huge grin from the moment that we entered until we left. And stories? Oh, did he have stories.

He remembered so much about Father Joe. Like his sisters, he was surprised, but "not really all that surprised, to tell you the truth," when he learned of Kathleen and Henry. He recalled the times that he spent with Father Joe on various Wisconsin lakes. He knew of his alcoholism and eventual sobriety.

The Father Joe that Jim knew was more of an Uncle Joe. Jim, his father, and Father Joe fished and boated on the lakes of southern Wisconsin. Father Joe belonged to various yacht clubs, and the guys enjoyed swimming and sailing together. On those recreational days, Jim was instructed to call him "Uncle Joe." He wanted to be a regular guy rather than A Priest.

Jim remembered Father Joe as a fun-loving man who had "a heckuva time" at all the reunions. "He had a beautiful bass singing voice," he recalled. He brought his own alcohol to these reunions, at times polishing off a bottle of gin a day. Father Joe's brother, Father Bob, also arrived with a traveling bar in tow, since their little sister didn't stock liquor at the Raddenbach farmhouse. In addition, both men usually traveled to family gatherings with their long-term housekeepers. The kids all knew Ginny. As Jim put it, "She was a knockout. And we knew not to ask questions."

According to Jim, at some point, Father Joe was sent to a Catholic rehabilitation center somewhere out west "to go and dry out. After that, he never touched liquor again." He retired at a relatively young age, 60, after having separated from Ginny, somewhere between Fond du Lac and his final, scandal-ridden assignment. He gradually became disabled with general weakness and liver disease. During the last 20 years of his life, Father Joe moved between various care facilities in the Milwaukee area. It was during a visit to one of these places that he told Jim that he wrote his autobiography in verse, and that it was not to be read by anyone until "after he'd gone." Unfortunately, neither Jim nor anyone else knew what became of this document. Jim longed to get his hands on a copy.

And then he pulled out the photo albums. I tried not to devour them too greedily. I tried to be interested in the Raddenbach parents and relatives. But, oh my heavens, there was Father Joe, playing on the floor with the kids! No clerical garb, he looked for all the world like anyone else.

"Yup, that's how he was," Jim said. I turned the page, and my heart leapt to my throat.

"Is this...?" I began, looking up, wide-eyed at Jim.

"Yup, that's Ginny. She was quite a looker. A real classy lady." There, tucked inconspicuously between other random snapshots, was a picture of Ginny. She sat on a sofa, squished between Father Joseph to and Jerome Raddenbach. Everyone appeared comfortable, like they were all used to each other and had no need for awkwardness. No one looked at the camera, they appeared ignorant of the photographer. Father Joe leaned back in the cushions. And Ginny—she looked happy. She smiled brightly, her lips stained a dark red and her hair curled. She was beautiful and glowing and happy. She still looked hopeful.

This photograph's existence was everything. I carefully lifted it from the sticky-backed album. "Joe, you have to get these pictures out of this 'magnetic' album, it'll ruin them!" I said. Over time, the pictures can permanently adhere to the sticky backing and plastic covering, trapping them. Luckily, this one came loose. I gently fed this precious relic through my portable scanner to be digitized. For good measure, I snapped a picture on my camera. I feared that this photo might somehow disappear, that it was a figment of a subconscious that thought about these two people for months on end. But it was real!

The afternoon was wonderful, and I couldn't wait for these warm, joking, lovely people to fold Henry and Kathleen into their embrace. And I couldn't wait to get home and get those photographs sent off. I felt guilty about being there in Henry's and Kathleen's absence and tried to temper my enthusiasm a bit.

From: Me
To: Henry Fetta, Kathleen LeFranc
I got together with a few of your cousins today—Kathy Witzack & Betty Link, both formerly Raddenbach, and their husbands, and Jim Raddenbach. Their mother, Veronica (Bier) Raddenbach, was Father Joe's sister. I had a couple things that I needed to return to Kathy, and she organized a luncheon for me and my mom. It was nice, and they are already brainstorming on how best to host a party whenever you, Kathleen, are visiting! You will really like them.

Jim brought along a few photo albums and I scanned photos of interest. The most amazing is one of Father Joe and Ginny sitting on a couch next to the Raddenbach's dad, Jerome Raddenbach, and one of the kids. There are also two of Father Joe on the floor playing with his nieces and nephews. I hope you are as thrilled with them as I am!

Fondly,
AB

From: Kathleen LeFranc
To: Me, Henry Fetta
Wow! The photos of Fr Joe with the kids are dated October '56....I turned 4 that month and Ginny was pregnant with Henry! Crazy stuff. Thank you for scanning these photos. Makes everything come to life. Love you, Angie!

From: Henry Fetta
To: Me, Kathleen LeFranc

Angie,
Thank you, having our mother and father next to each other in a picture is too much for words; who would have thought that one even existed, much less to find one. Lynn put together an album for me for Christmas and these will soon be included.

My family is touched by the resemblances in both Kathleen and me from both Fr. Joseph and Ginny; my children loved seeing a picture of their grandparents together. I think Ginny looks strikingly beautiful and cheerful in that picture and that's the way I want to always remember her. I think we can all better understand Jerome's sadness this summer for his dear sister that she was not able to find the right person in her life to raise a family, probably something she always wanted. My sense is that she would have loved reuniting with Kathleen and me, but we will have to wait until heaven for that.

As we close this year, I am so thankful for so many blessings that have been given to us. You, dear cousin, are the gift that just keeps on giving and giving....... Love, Henry

Henry's words were too kind. He and Kathleen gave me a gift. Most of the time, genealogists toil in silence and obscurity. It was a gift to share my work with an interested audience. I remain grateful to them, for letting me come along for the ride; for letting my dusty files, trees, photographs, and charts contribute to life-altering events; or giving this prematurely-retired pediatrician at loose ends a focus and daily work.

Candy Cane Cookies

1 C butter (or margerine)
2 t vanilla
1/2 C xx sugar
2 T water
2 1/2 C sifted flour

1/2 t almond flavoring
1 1/2 t salt
1 1/2 C Quaker oats
(uncooked)

Beat butter & vanilla until creamy. Add sugar gradually; beat until fluffy. Add water. Sift together flour & salt; add to creamed mixture, mixing thoroughly. Stir in oats until blended. (Dough will be quite stiff) Shape into canes. Place on ungreased cookie sheets. Bake in slow oven (325) 20 min. Cool. Frost with confectioner's sugar frosting. Stripe with thick red frosting. Makes 36

My Grandma Bier's recipe for candy cane cookies. Remember to ice them!

THE "SIMPLIFIED" TREE

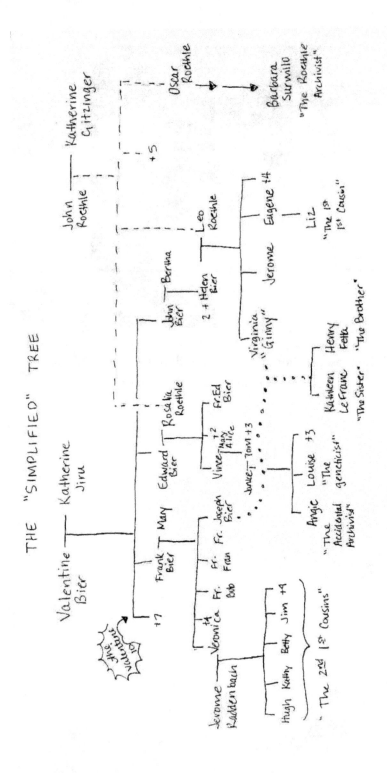

Father Joseph Bier, goofing around on the floor with his
Raddenbach nieces and nephews

Father Joseph Bier, Ginny Roethle, Jerome Raddenbach and daughter.

Chapter Twenty-One
Elephants in the Room

The story of Father Joe, Ginny, Henry, and Kathleen is a unique one. It has so many eyebrow-raising moments, and many twists and turns. If presented as a work of fiction, the reader would throw up their hands in annoyance at all of the coincidences and strokes of luck.

But it's real. As such, there are a few banal questions that inevitably bubble up. The questions are the elephants in the room, and it's time for these elephants to be acknowledged and ushered out.

What's the deal with priests' housekeepers?

Father Joe and Ginny maintained their illicit relationship within the context of a perfectly sanctioned one—that of a Roman Catholic priest and his housekeeper. But this sanctioned arrangement was neither clearly defined nor uniformly interpreted from rectory to rectory. In the example of Joe and Ginny, they lived together, alone, under the same roof. Ginny traveled with him to family functions, acting as a consort of sorts. The Raddenbach children wondered about the nature of their relationship, but never questioned it aloud to the adults. To what degree was this priest-housekeeper role an anomaly, and to what degree was it representative of a larger pattern in the Church?

Some answers can be found within the story of the Bier priests themselves. Father Joe's brother, Father Bob, also had a long-term housekeeper who traveled with him in much the same way that Ginny accompanied Father Joe. There is no evidence that Father Bob and his housekeeper's private relationship was romantic, but the public version closely mirrored that of Father Joe and Ginny. For the Raddenbach family, at least, the role of housekeeper as consort was an accepted one.

My great uncle, Father Ed Bier, employed a long-term housekeeper who inherited his entire estate, much to the ire of Ed's living brothers. They were especially put out about her keeping certain family mementoes. However, after she oversaw the changing of his will from his hospice bed, she possessed all the legal standing, if not the moral high ground. Ed's older brother, my Grandpa Vince, wanted to challenge the will in court. However, the other brother, Alfie, advised that it was best to let sleeping dogs lie, suggesting that perhaps they didn't want to closely examine the relationship in a court of law. So that's where the story ended. The relationship between Father Ed and his housekeeper was close enough that she ultimately controlled his estate. Romantic? Who knows. Excessively enmeshed? Definitely.

The original Bier priest, Father Charles, had the same housekeeper for most of his professional career. He took in his sister, Amalia, after she became a young widow with four children. This arrangement served the dual purpose of caring for his needs and providing room and board for an otherwise destitute family. The entire brood traveled between rectories with him, with Amalia serving as housekeeper and mother, creating an interesting facsimile of domestic life within the theoretically childless rectory walls.

Father Charles was allowed to house an entire family within the rectory because the hiring and firing, paying or underpaying of housekeepers was left entirely to priests' discretion. For so-called secular priests, those supervising parishes rather than residing in monasteries or church institutions, housekeepers were a completely unregulated, but necessary fixture.

Priests filled the positions with a variety of personalities in a variety of ways, always under the watchful eyes of their parishioners. Church members may have speculated on relationships in the form of idle gossip. Except, that is, at Father Joseph's final parish. There, the suspected indiscretion with his housekeeper (not Ginny) led to distribution of pamphlets, a libel suit, and his abrupt move into retirement. This was in the late 1960s, perhaps signaling a shift away from congregational indifferences to priests' personal lives.

Nowadays, churches still advertise for rectory housekeepers, although most of these are part-time, non-residential positions. And while the positions continue to exist, so does the scuttlebutt. On a blog titled *Catholic Truth,* a post in 2016 addresses the issue of how the writers should handle repeat allegations of a priest's housekeeper (noted to be a divorcee with children) behaving more like the lady of the house than an employee, with all the attendant implications. The author notes that ". . . we know that priests' housekeepers, like doctors' receptionists, can, indeed, get above themselves." (10)

In spite of the trope's existence, there is little scholarly work on the subject. Instead, there are random mentions in the popular press of priests' housekeepers, usually embracing one of these stereotypes rather than examining it. For example, a newspaper clipping on a retirement celebration paints the image of the happy, saintly housekeeper. The priest describes his lifelong housekeeper as "'... a second mother to me . . . She was a strong source of encouragement for me and always so kind and full of hope.'" (11).

The article's author contrasts this image of a willing saint with that of the nuns who were forced to work as unpaid servants, often in slave-like settings, to support larger religious institutions such as schools, seminaries, monasteries and abbeys. A particular example? That of the Sisters of St. Francis in Milwaukee. This group may sound familiar, having been mentioned as the caregivers both of Alverno College, home of Father Raymond Parr, and of St. Francis Seminary, attended by five Bier priests. Of these women, the author writes:

> Not all priests' housekeepers were happy, of course. There are sad cases of abuse and exploitation. In the nineteenth century, many nuns were required to serve priests and seminarians. The Sisters of St. Francis of Assisi of Milwaukee were made into servants of a seminary. They had to take turns living their rule. They described themselves as "crucified by their work." The seminarians complained about their cooking. The priests who directed them forced them to work without pay because of the debt on their house. (11).

Father Charles Bier's memoirs recall these Sisters in a far different manner, as willing helpmates to the seminarians, working to ensure their comfort and freedom from worldly concerns while pursuing a vocation. The truth probably lies somewhere in the middle.

One bit of scholarly work on the subject was written by a UCC student, Noirin Deady, and its title states her conclusions baldly: "Housekeepers for Priests were Exploited." While her original thesis is not in print, a review article explains that Ms. Deady based her work on interviews with a series of women who served as housekeepers for Irish parish priests as far back as the 1950s. One of her subjects began her career as a 13-year-old girl, sent by her mother to keep house for an unfamiliar priest. The reviewer summarizes Ms. Deady's findings on the unsanctioned role of housekeeper:

> She found exploitation in the form of long working hours, minimal pay and a lack of provision for old age and retirement. The priests neglected to register their stance as employers and those interviewed by Ms. Deady felt the job was a "vocation" and that housekeepers "'were as dedicated as any religious sister. It was convenient for priests to take that stance, most women did not choose to become housekeepers," she said. "They cooked, cleaned and carried out their chores and often looked after elderly and infirm priests, so there was also an overlap between domestic work and care work." (12)

So, what *is* the deal with priests and their housekeepers? The relationships were unregulated and, largely, unexamined. They became the stuff of whispers and cultural tropes. They ranged from mother figures to employees, from power-wielding gatekeepers to long-suffering indentured servants, from secret lovers to not-so-secret. Father Joe and Ginny fell at an extreme end of a spectrum, but their relationship was indeed part of a spectrum as opposed to an absolute outlier.

There must be other children of priests out there, right?

Obviously, yes. From popes that openly married in the Middle Ages to the scourge of pedophilia that the church is only now beginning to deal with in a serious fashion, there are myriad examples of the clerical position being abused. Part of that track record includes the often-unacknowledged children of priests.

That priests have fathered and continue to father children is not a surprise. Some of these children are the result of coercion and abuse, others the result of apparently consensual, yet secret relationships. The Roman Catholic Church in Ireland is more progressive in dealing with this reality. It acknowledges that these children exist, and established an organization to deal with their well being (13). The Irish Church published a statement of guiding principles centered on the central tenet that the welfare of the children comes first. In fact, there is a support and advocacy group for these children, called Coping International.

The Roman Catholic church writ large is not nearly so progressive. In an expose published by the *New York Times* in February, 2019, the Vatican revealed that it, too, had an official set of rules for priests who father children. Unlike the leadership of the Irish Catholic Church, the Vatican declined to make this document public. Further, while there is no official enumeration of the children fathered by priests, the existence of this document suggests that they are not rare. Coping International alone claims 50,000 members in 175 countries (13). And while the Vatican declines to share its guidelines, a spokesman shared that priests are instructed to prioritize the welfare of the "child of the ordained" and leave the priesthood. (15)

It is unclear when the Vatican began to officially recognize the "children of the ordained" and prioritize their welfare. Probably not during the era of Father Joe's and Ginny's relationship. Instead, Father Joe likely sought counsel from some other source on how best to deal with Ginny's pregnancies. While the church didn't have clear paths for the children of the ordained, there were many institutions of various levels of repute to "deal with" unwed Catholic women. During Ginny's pregnancy with Kathleen, she was placed with the Brummels, whose parish provided this service. How did Father Joseph know that St. Mary's, Evanston, was the place to take her? Was there a secret network of priestly knowledge of such matters? Similarly, we are not sure where Ginny spent her pregnancy with Henry. He was born in a Catholic hospital and adopted through a more standardized process, as opposed to Kathleen's adoption arranged by the McHugh family friend. The details of Ginny's second pregnancy remain elusive.

Should we be worried about the fact that Father Joseph and Ginny were second cousins who had children together? What are the health implications?

The two obviously knew that they were related. Was this another taboo that they brushed aside? Does this mean that Henry, Kathleen, and their kids are at risk for diseases? Long story short, no. After consultation with an eminently qualified genetic counselor, my sister Louise, this is a relatively easy one to answer.

When two related individuals procreate, there is always a chance that a harmful trait may be revealed in their offspring. This occurs when a matching set of bad recessive genes are combined in a child. Each parent contributes a previously hidden copy of the recessive gene. Recessive genes are wimpy and only express themselves when paired up. Two copies of a recessive gene mean that the recessive trait finally wins and its effects show up. If a person carries only one copy of a recessive gene plus another "normal" version of the gene? The normal version wins and masks the recessive version. Sometimes a recessive gene can be for an innocuous trait, such as color blindness. Other times, a recessive gene can be for a true mistake that causes bad health effects. Those are the genes that we worry about showing up when closely related individuals have children.

Why are recessive genes more likely to pair up in related people? Recessive genes tend to be pretty rare. Recessive genes hang out in certain populations, enriched by intermarriages through the years. It's only been in the past couple of hundred years or so that people started to seek out partners outside the confines of their home village, town, or group. The likelihood of a recessive gene finding a match, therefore, increases when two people from the same pool procreate. It's just a matter of the odds.

Childbearing between related individuals is called consanguinity. As Louise explained to me, the risks of consanguinity are borne *solely by the offspring of that union.* If a bad match-up of recessive genes were going to show up, it would show up in the kids of the consanguineous union. In this case, if Father Joe and Ginny each quietly carried a bad recessive gene from their common Valentine Bier lineage, and they each randomly passed on that bad actor to their kids, we would know it; Henry and Kathleen would have health problems.

Fortunately, Kathleen and Henry are, physically, completely unremarkable. And in medicine, unremarkable is a good thing to be. There was either no bullet for them to dodge lurking in the Valentine Bier gene pool, or they successfully dodged it. There's no increased risk for any genetic diseases in their descendants. At all. Case closed.

As for social norms, even in today's world, a union between second cousins is perfectly legal. Cousin marriage was only beginning to become taboo in the 1950s. So, while our modern eyebrows raise at a relationship between second cousins, that bit of the story was likely of little concern to either Joe and Ginny or their contemporaries.

A final open question, an elephant that I am unable to banish, is the very real possibility that Henry and Kathleen could have more siblings out there, just waiting for the right moment to submit their DNA to 23andme.

In fact, at the time of publication, an additional half-sibling fathered by Father Joseph Bier was identified by 23andme. But his story is his own to tell . . .

Epilogue

Since beginning to tackle this mystery almost a year ago, everything has changed and yet nothing has changed. Henry and Kathleen's "families of life" are the same. But they both have taken on a strange and wonderful new reality. From what they've told me, their own life families have been accepting, and their children grapple with the information in a variety of ways with varying degrees of success. That almost all the relationships and encounters throughout the story have been positive and warm is a testament to the innate kind hearts of Kathleen and Henry.

Father Joe and Ginny, the parents of these two generous souls, are buried 100 miles apart. The granular details of their lives will always remain mysteries. Each of us fill in the details with a combination of the memories of people who knew them, shadowy photographs, and our own hopes and dreams.

My sister, Louise, continues to advance her career in the world of genetic medicine in New York City. I don't get to see her nearly often enough, but we randomly call each other every couple of weeks or so and refuel our emotional tanks that way. As far as she knows, we are the only case that has used the Studbook Management software to solve a genetic genealogy mystery.

The field of genetic genealogy is having quite a moment, heralded by the much-publicized apprehension of the Golden State Killer. The media grabbed hold of the concept, and the term genetic genealogy entered the zeitgeist. Now, genetic genealogy is "a thing," something that I fell into accidentally.

23andme reported $65 million in revenue in 2018, and remains a privately-held company with 24 main investors. It holds the market share in private genetic testing technology, with Ancestry.com their main competitor. Kathleen sent them a brief synopsis of how "the spit was it" for her and Henry. She was contacted by their marketing department, who asked if she'd be willing to sit for an interview regarding the story. In exchange, they offered her one free test kit. She declined.

I took a trip back to St. Francis Xavier to photograph the cemetery. I didn't see Marilyn. I tried calling her to offer apologies and a chance to read this manuscript. She declined any further contact with either Henry or me.

The Archdiocese of Milwaukee may or may not know any of the details of this story in advance of this book's publication. Aside from the few inquiries I made to the diocesan archivist, I did not reveal the unfolding truth to them. The Roman Catholic Church writ large recently held a conclave to deal with the far more black-and-white issue of child sexual abuse by clergy. The gray-shaded issue of the variety of children of priests remains cloaked in secrecy.

The connection that I established with Father Joe's nieces and nephews from the Raddenbach family is taking root and hopefully will flourish. Betty (Raddenbach) Link is anxious to plan a get together with her siblings, Henry, and Kathleen, when Kathleen comes home to visit her Chicago family. The Raddenbach clan continues to welcome anyone touched by this story. I receive calls and emails from them occasionally, just to check in. After meeting my mother over the summer and again over Christmas, Kathy (Raddenbach) Witzack and her husband had my parents over for dinner and cards. They played Five Hundred, of course. They are looking to get another card party date on the calendar.

Liz, the first biologic cousin that Kathleen ever met, continues to work on Roethle family genealogy from her home in Florida. She is amazed that the time that she and Kathleen spent rummaging around online bore such remarkable fruit. She introduced several other extended Roethle family members to Henry and Kathleen, and these cousins provide additional nuance and depth to the story of the Roethles in general, and beautiful, tormented Ginny in particular.

The Rock County Biers continue to tear it up and get together in the converted pig barn for cards. I haven't widely divulged the story in advance of this book, lacking a clear platform, but the random cousins that I told seem interested. The general desire to delve into genealogy, as in so many families, varies widely. Auntie Eleanor remains in good health at age 86 and still lives alone in the Valentine Bier farmhouse. It will still likely be razed when she no longer requires it.

Kathleen is looking to secure a date for her next trip back to the Midwest, once the weather improves. While I don't get to see her as often as I do Henry, and our correspondence has trailed off as the mystery has resolved itself, she remains a friend and cousin that I know will be available to me, and I to her, at a moment's notice. She still baristas at Starbucks and peppers her correspondence with emojis.

Henry is retired from work, but devotes a great deal of his time to a nonprofit which secures protein-rich food for Chicago area food banks. He and Lynn also dote on their grandchildren. Henry hopes to pursue answers to other questions: How did Ginny manage to hide her pregnancy with him? Where did she stay? What was the relationship between Father Joe and Ginny like after leaving Francis Xavier? How did things end? Of course, he continues to pursue these questions with Henry-ish deliberation, and keeps me apprised of his progress.

As for me, the Accidental Archivist, after spending so much time on this mystery, I finished the manuscript that is now the book you are holding. I organized all the resulting information on the Bier family, and recently held a genealogy exchange in which I was able to meet many of the people with whom I corresponded on this and other matters. Henry and his oldest daughter attended, and I was thrilled to introduce them as the "Bierest of the Biers." I continue to work on genealogy, writing, taking care of the kids and volunteering. I plan to turn my attention to other branches of my tree in the months to come. To my husband and daughters, the completion of this project will not demonstrably change anything. There's always another mystery to solve, another page to write. They will always have cause to accuse me of caring too much about dead people. Of course, they are wrong, but I admit that it'll look that way sometimes.

I look forward to meeting the rest of Henry and Kathleen's children. Thrown together by circumstance and dumb luck, the three of us share a bond that I hope will last a lifetime. I remain grateful to Kathleen and Henry for allowing me to participate in their story. Genealogy is often a solitary pursuit. The work yields stacks of papers, documents, and photos. To be able to use all of the knowledge that I've squirreled away—both genealogical and medical—is a gift. And for that, I thank them.

Afterword

I personally want to thank Father Paul McArdle for bringing me into the most amazing family I could ever have imagined, the McHugh household. He is the only one besides Virginia and Father Joe who knew this entire story. As a young child, in order for me to grasp the concept of being adopted, my parents regularly read me a book called "The Chosen Baby" by Valentina P. Wasson. I truly am that Chosen Baby. Father Paul chose me. Not only was he my Dad's (George McHugh) first cousin and his dear friend, but also mine. He baptized me, married me, and baptized my children before he passed away. It appears, in my conversations with Henry, that he most likely helped Virginia and Father Joe when she was pregnant with Henry. Had my mother, Kathryn McHugh, not been pregnant with my brother, Dan McHugh, it's a strong possibility that Henry also would've been brought into our home. To that, we will never know. All I am sure of is his love for me and our family and for that I am eternally grateful.

To my brother, Bill (also adopted) and my brother Dan and sister Molly, thank you for your love.

My journey to discover who my genetic parents are began when I held my children in my arms for the very first time. That is when I understood unconditional love.

I love you all without condition. Thank you Angie!!! I'm looking forward to many years of new discoveries as we merge our families together.

-Kathleen McHugh, June 2022

I like to describe this story as both "miraculous" and "magical". "Miraculous" because so many pieces had to fall into place for Kathleen and me to find each other and our biological parents that it's impossible not to call our connection a miracle. Without the remarkable advancements in DNA testing, Kathleen's persistence and passion to understand her story and Angie's expertise and willingness to help us, this story would not have been told. And it's "magical" because Kathleen and I are now blessed not only to have one another but also to have truly remarkable extended families who have welcomed us into their lives. There is so much that lies ahead to enjoy together.

The true heroes of this story are my loving and caring parents, Henry and Mary Fetta (Blattner). They were married in May, 1952, and adopted me from St. Vincent's Orphanage in Chicago in May, 1957 ,when I was six weeks old. They were devoutly Catholic and gave me and my sister, Rita (also adopted from St. Vincent's in 1960), every opportunity to succeed. Henry was a carpenter and jack-of-all-trades; he built our home in Clarendon Hills, IL. Neither Henry nor Mary attended college and they wanted to make sure they gave us that chance. They made many sacrifices for us to attend Catholic grammar school and high school and ultimately to send me to the university of my choice. Mary passed away in 2004 and Henry died in 2011 and I am forever grateful of the unconditional love they bestowed on me.

Growing up I never had any curiosity about finding my biological parents and would never have searched because I knew it would have been hurtful to Henry and Mary. When Henry died, he left an envelope for me and Rita with our biological birth certificates and after I retired in 2013 I gave a search some thought. After being unsuccessful with my own on-line research, I hired a small search firm to do some digging for me. Their exploration was unproductive as they were using Betty Rohner as my birth mother's name and could not find any connections for me. I may have stopped there but two of my children gave me a 23andMe kit for my birthday in 2018 and here we are.

Being part of a story like this is a bit surreal and being the son of a Catholic priest and his beautiful, much younger second cousin who went to work for him as his housekeeper is a lot to process. While I am filled with joy in finding Ginny and Fr. Joe, my sadness lies in not getting to meet them to let them know we turned out just fine. Kathleen and I know they would have been proud of their children and would have loved the joy of being grandparents. I hold onto the belief that their story is one filled with love.

I am the benefactor of all of the research that Kathleen did to find our biological mother, Virginia Roethle, and all of the time and dedication that Angie took to help us identify and confirm our biological father, Fr. Joseph Bier, and to author this amazing manuscript. To them I will be forever grateful.

May God bless Ginny and Fr. Joe. Eternal rest grant unto them, O Lord, and let perpetual light shine upon them, may they rest in peace.

-Henry Fetta, January 2021

Sources

1.School Sisters of St. Francis. *Father Raymond A. Parr : priest of the Archdiocese of Milwaukee, WI, from 1939-2002.* SSSF Development Office. 2003. Alverno College Library. 282.092 P259f.

2.Kathleen LeFranc, personal conversation, May 12, 2018. Noted by Angela Bier.

3.Bernadette Link & James Raddenbach, personal conversation. August 13, 2018. Noted by Angela Bier.

4.Kathy Witzack, Betty Link, Henry Fetta, Jan Bier. Interview. August 30, 2018. Noted by Angela Bier.

5.Raynor Library-Archives. Marquette University. Collected works of Father Robert Gassert. UNIV C-1.17 Series 2.1-RGG

1.Box 1- General Correspondence

2.Box 3- Correspondence with Parents

6.Betz, Edna M. *If I Can You Can Decipher Germanic Records.* 1985.

7.St. Francis de Sales Seminary Website: https://www.sfs.edu/SFSHome

8.http://www.pastoralprovision.org/history.htm

9.https://www.aza.org/studbooks

10.https://catholictruthblog.com/tag/priests-housekeepers/ Catholic Truth Blog

11.https://www.ncronline.org/blogs/ncr-today/day-help Gerelyn Hollingsworth, National Catholic Reporter

12.https://www.irishexaminer.com/ireland/housekeepers-for-priests-were-exploited-study-147548.html#ixzz1UaHpjrKF Louise Roseingrave

13.http://www.copinginternational.com/ Coping International: Children of Priests and Religious.

14.https://www.bostonglobe.com/metro/2017/08/16/father-father-children-catholic-priests-live-with-secrets-and-sorrow/mvYO5SOxAxZYJBi8XxiaqN/story.html Michael Rezendes.

Boston Globe. August 16, 2017. "Children of Catholic priests live with secrets and sorrow"

15.https://www.nytimes.com/2019/02/18/world/europe/priests-children-vatican-rules-celibacy.html?action=click&modtule=Top%20Stories&pgtype=Homepagenn Jason Horowitz & Elizabeth Povoledo. NY Times. Feb. 19, 2019. "Vatican's Secret Rules for Priests That Have Children."

https://isogg.org/wiki/Autosomal_DNA_statistics